Brainteasers for the Commodore 64

Geneviève Ludinski
B.Sc.(Hons) A.M.B.C.S.

Phoenix Publishing Associates
Bushey, Herts.

Copyright © Geneviève Ludinski
All rights reserved

First published in Great Britain by
PHOENIX PUBLISHING ASSOCIATES
14 Vernon Road, Bushey, Herts. WD2 2JL

ISBN 0 9465 7609 2

Printed in Great Britain by
Billing & Sons Limited
Cover design by
David Berkoff
Typesetting by
Prestige Press (UK) Ltd.

INTRODUCTION

Before you dive into this book, here are a few tips you may find useful when keying in the programs.

You may miss out all the REM statements except the first two, and those containing the word 'subroutine'. These statements are just to help you understand how the program works. Also to save time and to ensure all the lines are fitted in, key in a question mark instead of PRINT. So, for example, key in ?X for PRINT X. If you have to correct a long line remember to change the PRINTs back to question marks.

Most of the programs use sound so remember to increase the volume on your television. Remember also to put in all the punctuation exactly as it appears. If you miss out a comma, the program may not work. If the program still does not work after you have corrected the errors reported by the computer, check the following. See whether you have confused any zeros for the letter O, or alternatively ones and the letter I. Check, also, that you have not missed any program lines. This is easily done if program lines look similar. Most program line numbers go up by ten at a time, so read your line numbers to find this one.

Some of the listings contain graphic characters so make sure that you press SHIFT and the appropriate key.

You may find some of the subroutines useful, and you are welcome to put these in any programs you write for your own use. You may not, of course, sell or give them away.

I hope you enjoy the book, and that your brain is not teased too heavily.

CONTENTS

Hexagon Puzzle	5
Safecracker	11
Spot the Difference	16
Saints to Sinners	23
Relations	29
Don't Paint the Cat	34
Sequence Countdown	39
What's Yours	44
Pattern Pairs	50
Concentration Test	56
Odd One Out	61
Decisive Hero	67
Western Adventure Game	75
Detective	81
Bar Charter	88
Stats Painter	93
Who Dunnit	99
Word Search	104
Fractions and Percentages	109
Francis Drake Adventure Game	115
A-Maze-Ing	128
Close Encounters of the Fourth Kind	133
Wire Maze	138

HEXAGON PUZZLE

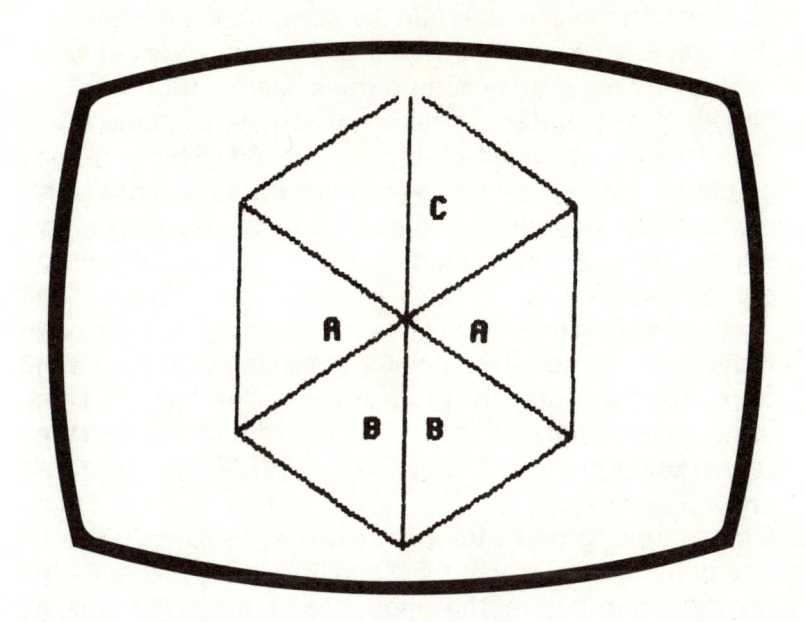

You are really up against the clock on this one as you must solve as many puzzles as possible, in just 200 seconds. A series of numbers, or letters, will be positioned around five of the sides of a hexagon and you will be asked to provide the missing letter or number. The relationship between the numbers or letters may be with their corresponding number or letter on the opposite side of the hexagon, or it may follow in sequence from an adjacent number.

The decision is yours.

How to play

Key in the number, or letter, of your choice and press RETURN key.

6

Programming hints

This program has a timer that displays the time in seconds on the screen while the computer is waiting for the player to key in something. This is a very useful facility and is done by setting the system variable TI$ to "000000" at the start of the program. TI will then hold the time in seconds multiplied by 60. This can be displayed on occasions throughout the program but is more effective being displayed constantly, especially when the program is waiting for the player to key in something. This is done by using GET in a loop which keeps checking if a key has been pressed and if it has not, it displays the time (see line 400). When a key has been found to be pressed, the program waits for the rest of the digits to be keyed and knows you have finished when the return key is pressed, i.e. GET I2$ = CHR$(13).

One change to make the puzzle easier, is to reduce the size of the numbers used. S(2) on line 140 is the value of the first number in the sequence if the pattern is a sequence of numbers going around the hexagon. IC on line 150 is related to the interval between the numbers going round the hexagon. So if the 9 in line 140 is changed to a smaller number and IC is always 1 this will make the puzzle easier.

If you wish to make the puzzle more difficult (and you must be brave or a genius to want to do so), then you could either increase the possible values of S(2) or IC or increase the number of different types of sequence. At present there are five different types of sequences depending on whether W is 0 to 4. If you allow W to become 5 or larger in line 160, you could add a new sequence type for W=5 after line 220.

Program

```
10 REM HEXAGON PUZZLE
20 REM COPYRIGHT (C) G.LUDINSKI 1983
30 HO$=CHR$(19):CL$=CHR$(147):CG$=CHR$(1
51):RD$=CHR$(28)
40 POKE53280,2:POKE53281,12:PRINTCG$;CL$
;
50 DIMS(8)
60 TE=0:CR=0:TI$="000000"
70 PRINTCL$;
80 TE=TE+1
90 IFTE=11ORTI>=12000THENGOTO620
100 REM
110 REM WORK OUT SEQUENCE
120 REM
130 S(1)=0
140 S(2)=INT(RND(1)*9+1)
150 IC=INT(RND(1)*4+1)
160 W=INT(RND(1)*5)
170 FORI=3TO8
180 IFW=0THENS(I)=INT(2*S(I-1)-S(I-2)+II
):GOSUB 730
190 IFW=1THENS(I)=INT(S(I-1)+S(I-2)+IC):
GOSUB740
200 IFW=2THENS(I)=INT(S(2)↑(I-1)):GOSUB7
50
210 IFW=3ANDI>5THENS(3)=S(2):S(4)=IC:S(5
)=INT((S(2)+IC)/2):GOSUB760
220 IFW=4ANDI>5THENS(3)=S(2):S(4)=IC:S(5
)=INT((S(2)+IC)/2):GOSUB790
230 NEXTI
240 REM
250 REM DISPLAY HEXAGON
260 REM
270 PRINT"                _____
                        /\      /\"
280 PRINT"               /  \   /  \
                      /    \ /    \"
290 PRINT"            /    \ /    \
                   /
```

```
                \"
300 PRINT"                  /_____V_____
_\                          \        ^
 /"
310 PRINT"                   \      / \
/                             \    /   \      /
"
320 PRINT"                     \  /     \    /
                                \/       \  /"
330 PRINT"                      V         V
                                 _____"
340 IFS(8))26THENLE=0:PRINTHO$;:PRINT:PR
INT:PRINTTAB(11);S(7);TAB(23);S(3):GOSUB
820
350 IFS(8)<=26THENLE=1:PRINTHO$:PRINT:PR
INTTAB(13);CHR$(64+S(7));:GOSUB830
360 REM
370 REM INPUT ANSWER
380 REM
390 IX=1
400 GETI$:IFI$=""THENPRINTHO$;INT(TI/60)
:GOTO400
410 PRINTTAB(16);I$;
420 GETI2$:IFI2$=""THENGOTO420
430 IFI2$=CHR$(13)THENGOTO450
440 I$=I$+I2$:PRINTI2$;:GOTO420
450 REM
460 REM CHECK ANSWER
470 REM
480 IFLE=0ANDABS(VAL(I$)-S(8))<=LEN(I$)/
2THENGOSUB860:GOTO560
490 IF LE <> 1 THEN GOTO 510
500 IFI$=CHR$(64+S(8))ORI$=CHR$(65+S(8))
THENGOSUB860:GOTO560
510 FORI=1TO6:PRINT:NEXT:PRINT"NO,THE AN
SWER = ";
520 IFLE=0THENPRINTS(8)
530 IFLE=1THENPRINTCHR$(64+S(8))
540 IFLE=1THENGOSUB880
550 PRINT:PRINTMS$
560 PRINT:PRINT"PRESS RETURN TO CONTINUE
"
```

```
570 INPUTA$
580 GOTO70
590 REM
600 REM SCORE SHEET
610 REM
620 PRINTCL$;:PRINT
630 PRINT"NUMBER OF PUZZLES COMPLETED =
";TE
640 PRINT:PRINT"NUMBER CORRECT = ";CR
650 PRINT:PRINT"TIME TAKEN = ";INT(TI/60
);" SECONDS"
660 IQ=INT(CR*100/5.3)
670 PRINT:PRINT"YOUR IQ LEVEL (NUMERACY)
 = ";IQ
680 PRINT
690 IFCR>=7THENPRINT"THIS IS CLASSED AS
SUPERIOR (UPPER 10%)":GOTO720
700 IFCR=6THENPRINT"THIS IS CLASSSD AS G
OOD (UPPER 20%)":GOTO720
710 IFCR=5THENPRINT"THIS IS CLASSED AS F
AIR (UPPER 60%)"
720 GOTO900
730 MS$="THE INTERVAL INCREASES BY "+STR
$(IC)+" EACH TIME":RETURN
740 MS$="EACH NUMBER IS THE SUM OF THE P
REVIOUS   TWO PLUS "+STR$(IC):RETURN
750 MS$="EACH NUMBER IS "+STR$(S(2))+" T
O THE POWER OF 2,3,4,5,6 AND 7":RETURN
760 MS$="EACH NUMBER IS"+STR$(S(2))+" TI
MES THE NUMBER     OPPOSITE IT"
770 S(I)=S(2)*S(I-3)
780 RETURN
790 S(I)=IC*S(11-I):MS$="THE NUMBERS ON
"
800 MS$=MS$+ "THE LEFT HAND SIDE OF THEH
EXAGON ARE"+STR$(IC)+" TIMES THE NUMBER"
810 MS$=MS$+"S ON THE   RIGHT HAND SIDE":
RETURN
820 PRINT:PRINTTAB(10);S(6);TAB(22);S(4)
:PRINTTAB(17);S(5):RETURN
830 PRINTTAB(25);CHR$(64+S(3)):PRINT:PRI
NTTAB(13);CHR$(64+S(6));TAB(25);CHR$(64+
S(4))
```

```
840 PRINTTAB(19);CHR$(64+S(5))
850 RETURN
860 PRINTRD$;" YES";CG$;:CR=CR+1
870 FORT=1TO11:PRINT:NEXT:RETURN
880 PRINT:PRINT"REPLACE EACH LETTER BY I
TS POSITION    NUMBER E.G. 1 FOR A,2 FO
R B..."
890 RETURN
900 END
```

SAFECRACKER

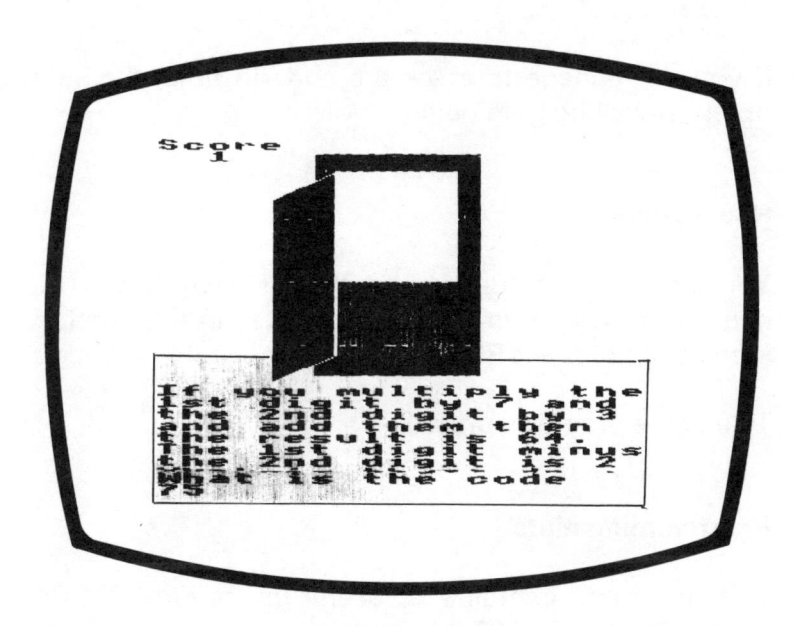

Are you a quick-thinker or a deep thinker? I hope you are one or the other, or you will never be able to crack open someone else's safe!

This game can be played two different ways, depending on whether you are a quick or deep thinker. If you are not sure which you are, then I suggest you play it both ways, and find out which way gives you the highest score.

In all cases, a closed safe is displayed and you are given two clues about the secret code that opens it. If you work out the exact answer before keying in the code, you are given 2 minutes to do it. If you make guesses, then you are only allowed 16 seconds. Wrong answers are ignored.

If you take too long you are surprised by the caretaker who switches on the light. He then presses the alarm button and you hear the police sirens wailing and you know all is lost.

If you do manage to crack the code in time, the safe opens, revealing gold bullion.

How to play

You are given two clues such as those shown above. The code is always a two digit number. Key in the number (you need not press RETURN).

To end the program, press E.

Programming hints

This program contains a useful procedure BLOCK subroutine at line 500 which draws a rectangle whose lower left hand corner is X,Y and whose width is W and height is H.

If you want to make the game easier, you can increase the time allowed to guess or reduce the number of digits allowed in the code or both.

To increase the time allowed for guesses, increase the value of TM in line 310. To increase the time allowed when only one answer is keyed in, increase the value of TM in line 290.

To reduce the number of digits allowed, reduce the number inside the RND brackets for XX and YY in line 660.

If you find the game too easy then do the opposite.

Program

```
10 REM SAFE CRACKER
20 REM COPYRIGHT (C) G.LUDINSKI 1983
30 POKE53280,11:POKE53281,0:REM BORDER A
ND BACKGROUND
40 POKE53272,21:REM UPPER CASE
50 CM=55296:PM=1024 : REM COLOUR AND SCR
EEN MAP
60 BL=0:RD=2:YE=7:WH=1
70 HO$=CHR$(19):CL$=CHR$(147):R1$=CHR$(1
8):R0$=CHR$(146):BL$=CHR$(144)
80 WH$=CHR$(5):CU$=CHR$(145):SQ$=CHR$(16
0):RD$=CHR$(28):GR$=CHR$(30)
90 SC=0
100 REM
110 PRINTWH$;
120 PRINTCL$;
130 PRINTHO$;"SCORE":PRINT" ";SC
140 REM
150 REM DRAW SAFE CLOSED
160 REM
170 CO=5:X=0:Y=24:W=40:H=8:GOSUB500
180 CO=WH:X=15:Y=16:W=10:H=15:GOSUB 500
190 PRINTHO$:PRINT:PRINT TAB(16);R1$;"__
_____"
200 FORI=1TO13:PRINTTAB(15);R1$;" |";TAB(
24);"| ":NEXT
210 PRINTR1$;TAB(16);"————————"
220 PRINTCU$;CU$;CU$;CU$;CU$;CU$;CU$;CU$
;R1$;TAB(22);"o"
230 TI$="000000"
240 GOSUB650
250 FORI=1TO8:PRINT:NEXT:PRINTR1$;GR$;"I
F YOU MULTIPLY THE 1ST DIGIT BY";A1;
260 PRINT" AND THE 2ND DIGIT BY ";ABS(B1
);"  AND ";S1$:PRINTR1$;GR$;"THE RESULT
IS ";C1;
270 PRINT".THE 1ST DIGIT ";S2$
280 PRINTR1$;GR$;"THE 2ND DIGIT IS ";C2;
".WHAT IS THE CODE"
```

```
290 TM=3600
300 GETI1$:IFTI<TMANDI1$=""THENGOTO300
310 IFI1$<>LEFT$(A$,1)ANDI1$<>"E"ANDTI<T
MTHENTM=480:GOTO300
320 IFI1$="E"THENGOTO820
330 IF T1 >= TM THEN GOTO 450
340 PRINTR1$;GR$;I1$;
350 GETI2$:IFTI<TMANDI2$=""THENGOTO350
360 IFI2$<>RIGHT$(A$,1)ANDTI<TMTHENGOTO3
50
370 IFTI>=TMTHENGOTO450
380 PRINTR1$;GR$;I2$;
390 I$=I1$+I2$
400 IFI$=A$THENSC=SC+1:GOSUB750
410 GOTO100
420 REM
430 REM SWITCH LIGHT ON AND PLAY POLICC
SIREN SOUNDS
440 REM
450 PRINTR1$;GR$;"NO,THE CODE IS ";A$:PO
KE53281,7:GOSUB830
460 FORI=1TO100:GETRB$:NEXT
470 POKE53281,0
480 GOTO100
490 REM
500 REM BLOCK SUBROUTINE - DEFINE X,Y,W,
H,CO
510 FORY1=Y-H+1 TO Y
520 FOR X1=X TO X+W-1
530 SD=(Y1*40)+X1
540 POKE CM+SD,CO
550 POKE PM+SD,160
560 NEXT
570 NEXT
580 RETURN
590 REM DOOR OPEN
600 PRINTWH$;HO$:PRINT:PRINT:PRINTTAB(14
);R1$;"▼"
610 CO=WH:X=14:Y=15:W=1:H=12:GOSUB500
620 FORI=1TO12:PRINT:NEXT
630 PRINTWH$;TAB(14);"▼"
640 RETURN
```

```
650 REM QUESTION
660 A1=INT(RND(1)*8+2):B1=INT(RND(1)*8+2
):XX=INT(RND(1)*10):YY=INT(RND(1)*10)
670 W1=(-1)↑INT(RND(1)*2+1):W2=(-1)↑INT(
RND(1)*2+1)
680 B1=B1*W1
690 C1=(A1*XX)+(B1*YY)
700 C2=XX+(W2*YY)
710 S1$="ADD THEM THEN":IFW1=-1THENS1$="
SUBTRACT THEM"
720 S2$="PLUS ":IFW2=-1THENS2$="MINUS"
730 A$=RIGHT$(STR$(ABS(XX)),1)+RIGHT$(ST
R$(ABS(YY)),1)
740 RETURN
750 REM OPEN SUBROUTINE
760 GOSUB590
770 CO=BL:X=16:Y=10:W=8:H=8:GOSUB500
780 CO=YE:X=16:Y=15:W=8:H=6:GOSUB500
790 PRINTHO$:PRINTWH$;TAB(1);SC
800 FORI=1TO1000:GETRB$:NEXT
810 RETURN
820 END
830 REM POLICE SIREN SUBROUTINE
840 GOSUB910
850 FORI=1TO10
860 POKE54273,38:POKE54272,126:FORT=1TO3
00:NEXT
870 POKE54273,34:POKE54272,75:FORT=1TO30
0:NEXT
880 NEXT
890 GOSUB950
900 RETURN
910 REM SOUND ON SUBROUTINE
920 POKE54296,15:POKE54277,190:POKE54278
,248
930 POKE54276,17
940 RETURN
950 REM SOUND OFF SUBROUTINE
960 POKE54276,0:POKE54277,0:POKE54278,0
970 RETURN
```

SPOT THE DIFFERENCE

I suppose that this could have been called Star and Stripe, the difference as you will see when you run this colourful eye test.

Two pictures, composed of stars and stripes, in different colours appear on the screen, and you will be asked to identify which of the items is different.

How to play

Items are keyed as follows:

        Blue Stripe   1
        Yellow stripe 2

Red stripe	3
Black star	4
White star	5
Red star	6

Identify the differences and key in the number and press RETURN. If you are correct you will hear a high pitched tune, but if you are wrong your answer will be crossed.

To help you, numbers previously keyed in are displayed in brackets. When all the numbers required have been keyed in a further tune will be played. Just hope that it is high pitched for a correct answer.

To continue, or stop, press Y or N and RETURN.

At conclusion you will see your score sheet showing tries, correct answers, and time/average taken.

Programming hints

You might find the subroutines at line 1070 and 1210 useful in your non-commercial programs as it draws a star. You just have to specify the bottom left-hand corner of the star (X,Y), and colour that it is to be displayed in (CL).

You could make the puzzle easier by increasing the range of possible values for the shapes that are going to be different. The function FNM (MAX) is used to define the minimum and maximum value of any shape. Remember if you increase the MAX value you must reduce MIN by the same value, or the picture will extend beyond the allocated area.

Program

```
10 REM SPOT THE DIFFERENCE
20 REM COPYRIGHT (C) G.LUDINSKI 1983
30 POKE53280,2:POKE53281,12:POKE53272,21
:REM BORDER BACKGROUND AND UPPER CASE
40 S1=54273:S2=54272:REM SOUND VARIABLES
50 HO$=CHR$(19):CL$=CHR$(147):CG$=CHR$(1
51):CU$=CHR$(145):CD$=CHR$(17)
60 BL$=CHR$(31):YE$=CHR$(158):RD$=CHR$(2
8):BK$=CHR$(144):WH$=CHR$(5)
70 CM=55296:PM=1024:KL=40:REM COLOUR AND
 SCREEN MAP
80 DIMWH(6),AN$(6)
90 V=53248:POKEV+21,63:REM ENABLE SPRITE
S
100 FORK=0TO5:POKE2040+K,13:NEXT:REM SPR
ITE DATA AREA
110 GOSUB1210
120 TI$="000000":CR=0:NQ=0
130 REM
140 REM RANDOM NUMBER IN RANGE
150 REM
160 DEF FNM(MAX)=INT((MAX-MIN)*RND(1)+MI
N)
170 REM
180 REM START
190 REM
200 PRINTCL$;CG$;
210 NQ=NQ+1
220 REM
230 REM FRAMEWORK
240 REM
250 PRINT   "┌─────────────────┐ ┌─────
───────┐"
260 A$=     "│                 │ │     
      │"
270 B$=     "└─────────────────┘ └─────
───────┘"
280 FORK=1TO16:PRINTA$:NEXT:PRINTB$
290 REM
```

```
300 REM DRAW PATTERNS
310 REM
320 NZ=0
330 FORI=1TO6
340 WH(I)=INT(2*RND(1))
350 IFWH(I)=1THENNZ=NZ+1
360 NEXTI
370 IFNZ=0THENGOTO330
380 MX=0
390 FORS=0TO1
400 FORJ=1TO3
410 IFS<>0THENGOTO480
420 X=6*(J-1)
430 MIN=3:W=FNM(4)
440 IJ=J
450 CL=J+5:IFCL=8THENCL=2
460 GOSUB990
470 X=X+20:MIN=1:W=W+WH(IJ)*FNM(2):GOSUB990
480 IFS<>1THENGOTO580
490 MIN=24:X=FNM(90)
500 MIN=50:Y=FNM(100)
510 IJ=J+3
520 CL=J-1
530 JC=J
540 GOSUB1070
550 JC=J+3
560 X=X+160:IFX>=255THENMX=MX+2↑(J+2):X=X-255
570 Y=Y+(WH(J+3)*60):GOSUB1070
580 NEXTJ
590 NEXTS
600 REM
610 REM QUESTION
620 REM
630 PRINTHO$:FORK=1TO18:PRINTCD$;:NEXT
640 PRINTTAB(10);"WHICH ARE DIFFERENT?"
650 RI$=CHR$(161)
660 PRINTSPC(7);BL$;"1. ";RI$;SPC(7);YE$;"2. ";RI$;SPC(7);RD$;"3. ";RI$
670 PRINTSPC(7);BK$;"4. *";SPC(7);WH$;"5. *";SPC(7);RD$;"6. *";CG$
680 GOSUB1120
```

```
690 IR$=""
700 FORI=1TO(LEN(A$)+1)/2
710 GETI$:IFI$=""THENGOTO710
720 PRINTI$;" (PREVIOUS GUESSES=";IR$;")
";
730 KI=0
740 FORK=1TONA
750 IFI$=AN$(K)THENAN$(K)="0":KI=1:GOSUB
1540:IR$=IR$+I$
760 NEXTK
770 IFKI=0THENPRINT" X":GOSUB1590:GOTO79
0
780 PRINT
790 PRINTCU$;"
    ":PRINTCU$;
800 NEXTI
810 FORI=1TONA
820 IFAN$(I)<>"0"THENGOTO850
830 NEXTI
840 GOTO860
850 PRINT"NO,ANS.=";A$:GOSUB1590:GOTO870
860 PRINT"YES,YOU ARE RIGHT":GOSUB1540:G
OSUB1540:CR=CR+1
870 PRINT"DO YOU WANT MORE Y/N";
880 INPUTR$
890 IFR$<>"N"THENGOTO200
900 REM
910 REM SCORE SHEET
920 REM
930 PRINTCL$:FORI=1TO12:PRINT:NEXTI
940 PRINT:PRINT"PUZZLES ATTEMPTED=";NQ
950 PRINT:PRINT"PUZZLES CORRECT=";CR
960 PRINT:PRINT"TIME TAKEN=";INT(TI/60);
"SECS"
970 IFCR<>0THENPRINT:PRINT"TIME PER CORR
ECT PUZZLE=";INT(TI/(CR*60));"SECS"
980 GOTO1650
990 REM STRIPE SUBROUTINE
1000 FORX1=XTOX+W-1
1010 FORY1=0TO17
1020 SD=(Y1*KL)+X1
1030 POKECM+SD,CL
```

```
1040 POKEPM+SD,160
1050 NEXT:NEXT
1060 RETURN
1070 REM STAR SUBROUTINE
1080 POKEV+38+JC,CL
1090 POKEV+2*(JC-1),X:POKEV+16,MX
1100 POKEV+(2*JC)-1,Y
1110 RETURN
1120 REM ANSWER SUBROUTINE
1130 A$="":IM=0
1140 FORL=1TO6
1150 IFWH(L)=1THENIM=IM+1:AN$(IM)=RIGHT$
(STR$(L),1):A$=A$+AN$(IM)+","
1160 NEXTL
1170 A$=LEFT$(A$,LEN(A$)-1)
1180 NA=IM
1190 RETURN
1200 REM
1210 REM READ SPRITE SUBROUTINE
1220 RESTORE
1230 FORS=0TO62
1240 READ SP
1250 POKE832+S,SP
1260 NEXT
1270 GOTO1490
1280 DATA 0,16,0
1290 DATA 0,56,0
1300 DATA 0,56,0
1310 DATA 0,124,0
1320 DATA 0,124,0
1330 DATA 0,254,0
1340 DATA 0,254,0
1350 DATA 1,255,0
1360 DATA 255,255,254
1370 DATA 127,255,252
1380 DATA 63,255,248
1390 DATA 31,255,240
1400 DATA 15,255,224
1410 DATA 7,255,192
1420 DATA 15,255,224
1430 DATA 15,255,224
1440 DATA 31,239,240
```

```
1450 DATA 31,199,240
1460 DATA 63,1,248
1470 DATA 60,0,120
1480 DATA 112,0,28
1490 RETURN
1500 REM SOUND ON SUBROUTINE
1510 POKE54296,15:POKE54277,190:POKE54270,248:POKE54276,17:RETURN
1520 REM SOUND OFF SUBROUTINE
1530 POKE54276,0:POKE54277,0:POKE54278,0:RETURN
1540 REM RIGHT-SOUND SUBROUTINE
1550 GOSUB1500
1560 POKES1,68:POKES2,149:FORTT=1TO200:NEXTTT
1570 GOSUB1520
1580 RETURN
1590 REM WRONG-SOUND SUBROUTINE
1600 GOSUB1500
1610 POKES1,45:POKES2,198:FORTT=1TO200:NEXTTT
1620 POKES1,43:POKES2,52:FORTT=1TO100:NEXTTT
1630 GOSUB1520
1640 RETURN
1650 END
```

SAINTS TO SINNERS

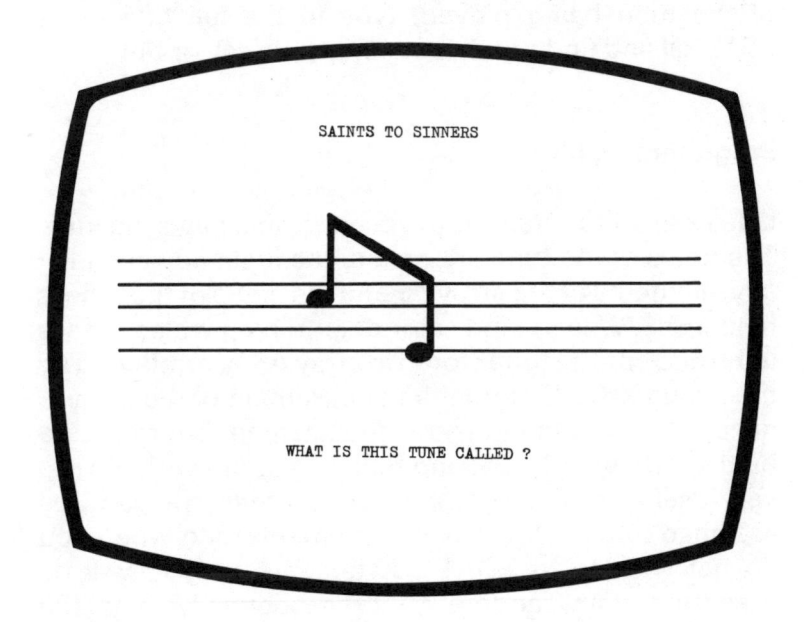

Here is a musical test for the members of your family who have a keen ear for a tune.

The object of the game is to guess the tune being played and to make it easy, to begin with, we have allowed your computer to play the entire tune. After the first ten 'numbers' you will only hear a short snatch from the tune.

We have included a very large selection of tunes suitable for 'saints and sinners'.

To make life more difficult for the player we have entered the tunes, using a special code, so that they cannot be guessed at in advance.

24

How to play

When you think that you have guessed, correctly, the title of the tune being played, type in the full title press RETURN and find out if your ear is musical, or tin.

Programming hints

Lines 230-740 contains the procedure that plays the tune. The notes of the tune are held in the first and second, if any, elements of the array A$ and the name of the tune is held in N$. W is the indicator determining which tune is to be played. The tune stored in array A$ is terminated by the letters XXX. If more than one element of the array is needed to store the tune, the first element is terminated by the letters NNN. Storing data in a string variable is a very useful trick when there are too many fields to be assigned to use assignment statements, and when you do not wish to use DATA statements, as you will be accessing data randomly, not sequentially. See the section entitled Possible alterations for further details.

The obvious alteration that can be made, are that when you know the names of the tunes you will want to change them. If you wish to increase the number of tunes that can be played then you must increase the maximum value of W held in line 130. You could then include your tune between 610 and 620 starting with a statement ensuring that the tune is skipped over if the value of W is not the correct one. You could then work out the tune your require on an instrument, or else you could copy a musical score. If you are copying a musical score then you should refer to the User Guide, but if you are doing it for fun then I recommend a child's musical instrument which usually just has the octave that starts with middle C which is the most common octave. The pitch numbers for this octave are:

Middle   C 1
               D 2
               E 3
               F 4
               G 5
               A 6
               B 7
               C 8
               and the A below Middle C 9

The duration of the notes should be smaller numbers than specified in the User Guide as processing the array takes time. Therefore I suggest that the durations should be 05,10 and 20 approximately for notes of short, middle or long duration. When you have worked out the pitch and duration of all the notes, you should assign them to the first and, if more room is required, the second element of the array A$. The pitch number must have one digit and the duration must have two and they should be joined together and separated from details of the next note by a space. As stated before, the first element is terminated by NNN and the second element by XXX.

I do not expect you will bother to put the name of the tune in code, but in case you do N$ is made up of the ASCII values of the letters of the name of the tune, remembering to include spaces which have an ASCII value of 32. If you do not bother to code the name of the tune, assign the name to NAM$ and make sure the program skips line 150.

Program

```
10 REM SAINTS TO SINNERS
20 REM COPYRIGHT (C) G.LUDINSKI 1983
30 POKE53280,2:POKE53281,12:POKE53272,21
:REM BORDER,BACKGROUND AND UPPER CASE
40 DIMA$(2),M(9,2)
```

```
50 HO$=CHR$(19):CL$=CHR$(147):CG$=CHR$(1
51)
60 NT=0
70 PRINTCL$;CG$;
80 POKE54296,15:POKE54277,190:POKE54278,
240:POKE54276,33:REM SOUND ON
90 NT=NT+1
100 PRINT:PRINT"             SAINTS TO SI
NNERS":PRINT:PRINT
110 GOSUB810
120 GOSUB750
130 W=INT(RND(1)*5)
140 GOSUB230
150 NAM$="":FORI=1TOLEN(N$)STEP2:NAM$=NA
M$+CHR$(VAL(MID$(N$,I,2))):NEXTI
160 PRINT:PRINT:PRINT:PRINT"       WHAT
IS THIS TUNE CALLED ?":PRINT
170 INPUTI$
180 IFI$=NAM$THENPRINT:PRINT"YOU ARE RIG
HT":GOTO200
190 PRINT:PRINT"NO,IT IS CALLED ":PRINTN
AM$
200 PRINT:PRINT"DO YOU WANT MORE Y/N"
210 INPUTR$:IFR$="Y"ORR$=""THENGOTO70
220 GOTO890
230 REM TUNE SUBROUTINE
240 A$(1)="":A$(2)="":N$=""
250 IFW<>0THENGOTO310
260 A$(1)="205 515 615 725 005 705 810 0
01 805 710 505 710 "
270 A$(1)=A$(1)+"610 005 205 320"
280 A$(1)=A$(1)+" 520 001 510 605 705 31
0 615 805 720 620 525"
290 A$(1)=A$(1)+" 005 XXX "
300 N$="8076657383738232683965777985B2"
310 IFW<>1THENGOTO410
320 A$(1)="110 210 310 110 010 "
330 A$(1)=A$(1)+"110 210 310 110 010 "
340 A$(1)=A$(1)+"310 410 520 005 "
350 A$(1)=A$(1)+"310 410 520 005 NNN "
360 A$(2)="505 605 505 405 310 110 010 "
370 A$(2)=A$(2)+"505 605 505 405 310 110
 010 "
```

```
380 A$(2)=A$(2)+ "110 910 120 010 "
390 A$(2)=A$(2)+ "110 910 120 010 XXX "
400 N$="708269826932746567818569B3"
410 IFW<>2THENGOTO470
420 A$(1)="305 205 110 205 305 405 510 0
05 605 705 810 "
430 A$(1)=A$(1)+"710 610 510 010 "
440 A$(1)=A$(1)+"605 705 810 710 610 510
 610 710 810 510 "
450 A$(1)=A$(1)+"410 310 010 XXX "
460 N$="84726932707382838432787969776"
470 IFW<>3THENGOTO530
480 A$(1)="110 001 310 001 420 005 405 0
01 405 305 405 510 001 "
490 A$(1)=A$(1)+"510 420 005 "
500 A$(1)=A$(1)+"410 610 810 005 605 001
 605 505 402 001 "
510 A$(1)=A$(1)+"402 305 420 XXX "
520 N$="7978676932737832827989657632686 5
8673683983326773848 9"
530 IFW<>4THENGOTO620
540 A$(1)="305 001 305 410 520 001 405 3
05 210 001 210 "
550 A$(1)=A$(1)+"305 001 305 "
560 A$(1)=A$(1)+"410 520 010 305 001 305
 410 520 001 405 "
570 A$(1)=A$(1)+"305 "
580 A$(1)=A$(1)+"210 001 210 305 001 305
 410 620 NNN "
590 A$(2)="010 510 610 820 001 805 705 6
10 001 610 005 "
600 A$(2)=A$(2)+"505 405 310 001 310 XXX
 "
610 N$="746932843965737769"
620 IFNT>10THENA$(1)=RIGHT$(A$(1),4*INT(
RND(1)*17+3))
630 FORJ=1TO2
640 FORI=1TO255STEP4
650 IFMID$(A$(J),I,3)="NNN"THENI=255:GOT
O710
660 IFMID$(A$(J),I,3)="XXX"THENI=255:J=2
:GOTO710
```

```
670 IFMID$(A$(J),I,1)="0"THENPOKE54296,0
:GOTO700
680 POKE54296,15
690 POKE54273,M(VAL(MID$(A$(J),I,1)),1):
POKE54272,M(VAL(MID$(A$(J),I,1)),2)
700 FORT=1TOVAL(MID$(A$(J),I+1,2))*20:NE
XTT
710 NEXTI
720 NEXTJ
730 POKE54276,0:POKE54277,0:POKE54278,0
740 RETURN
750 REM DRAW PICTURE SUBROUTINE
760 S1$="              "
770 PRINTS1$;"                         ":
    PRINTS1$;"―――――――――――――――――――――――――"
780 PRINTS1$;"―――――――――――――――――――――――――":
    PRINTS1$;"―――――――――――――――――――――――――"
790 PRINTS1$;"―――――――――――――――――――――――――":
    PRINTS1$;"―――――――――――――――――――――――――"
800 RETURN
810 REM READ NOTE VALUE SUBROUTINE
820 RESTORE
830 FORI=1TO9
840 READHI,LO
850 M(I,1)=HI:M(I,2)=LO
860 NEXT
870 DATA 34,75,38,126,43,52,45,198,51,97
,57,172,64,188,68,149,28,214
880 RETURN
890 END
```

RELATIONS

```
           Relations

        5  3  5  6
        3  2  1  2
        8  2  5  7   16
        7  1  8  7

     combine a row or column to be
         equal to the red number
        Use + - * / ∧ SQR < >
```

This following program is one where you should deny yourself, and any other player, the use of paper and pencil if you really want some mental exercise.

The screen will display a four by four matrix of numbers, to the left hand side. On the right hand side will be shown a number, or numbers, in red.

You have to combine two, or more, of the numbers in any of the rows to arrive at the same figure as the red number/s.

How to play

To reach your answer you may use any of the following operators:

+ plus
− minus
* multiplication
/ division
↑ to the power of
sqr square root of

Example: If the red number is 1 and the row is 9 2 4 8 the solution would be

SQR (9) + 2 − 4

This, followed by RETURN, would give 1 as it's answer. Then type cont then press RETURN.

Correct answers will mean that you will be asked if you wish to proceed. Answer Y or No followed by RETURN.

If you answer incorrectly your computer will tell you first.

A score sheet appears after 200 seconds which will show your results and give an IQ rating against your reasoning powers.

Programming hints

This program evaluates the expression keyed in by poking a question mark into the keyboard STOPping at line 440. Then the player keys in the expression, so the player is in fact printing the answer. This is read by PEEKing the screen in line 460 after the program has been CONTinued.

If you wish to increase the number of rows or columns of the matrix then you must change the maximum value of I (row) or J (column) in the FOR . . . NEXT loops.

Program

```
10 REM RELATIONS
20 REM COPYRIGHT (C) G.LUDINSKI 1983
30 POKE53280,2:POKE53281,12:REM BORDER A
ND BACKGROUND
40 POKE53272,23:REM LOWER CASE
50 HO$=CHR$(19):CL$=CHR$(147):RD$=CHR$(2
8):CG$=CHR$(151):CU$=CHR$(145)
60 DIM A(4,4),X(16),Y(16)
70 PRINTCL$;CG$;
80 TI$="000000":NO=0:CR=0
90 REM
100 REM GENERATE NUMBERS
110 REM
120 PRINTCL$;
130 IFTI>=12000THENGOTO750
140 NO=NO+1
150 FORI=1TO4
160 FORJ=1TO4
170 A(I,J)=INT(RND(1)*9+1)
180 NEXTJ
190 NEXTI
200 REM
210 REM DISPLAY NUMBERS
220 REM
230 FORI=1TO4
240 PRINT
250 FORJ=1TO4
260 PRINT" ";A(I,J);
270 NEXTJ
280 PRINT
290 NEXTI
300 REM
310 REM GENERATE RED NUMBER
320 REM
330 S1=INT(RND(1)*2+1):S2=INT(RND(1)*10)
:SM=VAL(STR$(S1)+RIGHT$(STR$(S2),1))
340 PRINTRD$;
350 PRINTHO$:FORI=1TO2:PRINT:NEXT:PRINTT
AB(20);SM
```

```
360 PRINTCG$;
370 REM
380 REM CHECK ANSWER
390 REM
400 FORI=1TO5:PRINT:NEXT
410 PRINT"-OMBINE A ROW OR COLUMN TO BE EQUAL TO   THE RED NUMBER"
420 PRINT
430 PRINT"IYPE EXPRESSION USING + - * / () / ↑ SQRTHEN _ETURN,THEN TYPE CONT _ETURN"
440 POKE631,63:POKE198,1:STOP
450 FORI=0TO11:POKE(55896+I),12:POKE(55936+I),12:POKE(56096+I),12:NEXT
460 EV=VAL(CHR$(PEEK(1745))+CHR$(PEEK(1746))+CHR$(PEEK(1747))+CHR$(PEEK(1748)))
470 I$="":FORI=0TO39:I$=I$+CHR$(PEEK(1705+I)):NEXT
480 IFI$=""THENGOSUB870:GOTO690
490 N$="":OP$=""
500 FORI=1TOLEN(I$)
510 NU$=MID$(I$,I,1)
520 IFNU$>="0"ANDNU$<="9"THENN$=N$+NU$:GOTO530
530 NEXTI
540 IFEV<>SMTHENPRINT:PRINT"/O,THEY ARE NOT=";SM:GOTO 690
550 IFLEN(N$)>40RLEN(N$)=0THENGOSUB870:GOTO690
560 SG$=""
570 FORT=1TO2
580 FORI=1TO4
590 SG$=SG$+"X"
600 FORJ=1TO4
610 IFT=1THENSG$=SG$+RIGHT$(STR$(A(I,J)),1)
620 IFT=2THENSG$=SG$+RIGHT$(STR$(A(J,I)),1)
630 NEXTJ
640 NEXTI
650 SG$=SG$+"X"
660 NEXTT
```

```
670 GOSUB900:IFIS=0THENGOSUB870:GOTO690
680 PRINT:PRINT" ES,YOU ARE RIGHT":CR=CR
+1
690 PRINT:PRINT" O YOU WANT MORE Y/N";
700 INPUTR$
710 IFR$<>"N"THENGOTO120
720 REM
730 REM SCORE SHEET
740 REM
750 PRINTCL$;
760 TM=TI/60
770 PRINT:PRINT" UMBER OF PROBLEMS =";NO
780 PRINT:PRINT" UMBER CORRECT = ";CR
790 PRINT:PRINT" IME TAKEN = ";INT(TM);"
 SECS"
800 IFTM<200THENGOTO960
810 IQ=INT((CR*100)/5.3):IFIQ>150THENIQ=
150
820 PRINT:PRINT"  LEVEL (REASONING)=";I
Q
830 IFCR>=7THENPRINT:PRINT" HIS IS SUPER
IOR    (UPPER 10%)":GOTO960
840 IFCR=6THENPRINT:PRINT" HIS IS GOOD (
UPPER 30%)":GOTO960
850 IFCR>=4THENPRINT:PRINT" HIS IS FAIR
(UPPER 60%)":GOTO960
860 GOTO960
870 REM ERROR SUBROUTINE
880 PRINT" RROR,WRONG NUMBERS"
890 RETURN
900 REM NUMBER CHECK SBROUTINE
910 IS=0
920 FORT=1TOLEN(SG$)
930 IFN$=MID$(SG$,T,LEN(N$))THENIS=1:GOT
O950
940 NEXTT
950 RETURN
960 END
```

DON'T PAINT THE CAT

```
IS THE FIRST NOTE IN THE TUNE HIGHER OR
LOWER THAN THE 2ND NOTE ?

PRESS H OR L
```

Seems a strange title for a program. I mean, who would want to emulsion paint the family mogg anyway?

Well you see, the family have decided that you have to paint the garden fence. You lost the draw — it might have been your sister instead who had to do it, but never mind there is always next time. Across the fence from you and your fantastic paint brush, is your neighbour's transistor. As a mental challenge you have decided to paint the fence according to the high/low pitch of your neighbour's music.

Look out for your cat, it's parked at the end of the fence.

How to play

As the game begins you will hear just two notes to compare but, everytime you get the answer correct the next tune will have an extra note.

You will be told which two notes to compare, and you must key in H or L for High or Low.

If you get it wrong you must wait for the fence, and the poor old pussy, to be painted.

If you take too long to answer, the cat will wind up getting covered in paint anyway.

Press the RETURN key when you want a new tune.

Programming hints

If you can work out the answer long before the cat is painted, then reduce the 34 in line 650 to 31.

If you find that it is too difficult to tell the difference between the notes, then change the 5 in line 120 to 10.

Alternatively you can increase the time allowed to answer, or reduce the difference between the notes, by doing the opposite of what is described above.

Program

```
10 REM DON'T PAINT THE CAT
20 REM COPYRIGHT (C) G.LUDINSKI 1983
30 POKE53280,5:POKE53281,6:POKE53272,21:
REM BORDER,BACKGROUND AND UPPER CASE
40 DIMN(14),T(14),C(2),P$(11)
50 HO$=CHR$(19):CL$=CHR$(147):CG$=CHR$(1
```

```
51):RD$=CHR$(28):WH$=CHR$(5)
60 CD$=CHR$(17):R1$=CHR$(18):R0$=CHR$(14
6):CU$=CHR$(145)
70 CM=55296:PM=1024:REM COLOUR AND SCREE
N MAP
80 S$="                                        "
90 KL=40
100 GOSUB910
110 DEF FNRN(A)=INT(RND(1)*A+1)
120 DEF FNRA(A)=INT(RND(1)*15)*5+1
130 PRINTCL$;WH$;
140 REM
150 REM CAT SHAPE
160 REM
170 P$(1)= "    /\_/\         ":
    P$(2)= "    |   |         "
180 P$(3)= "    | . . |       "
    :P$(4)= "    \ . /         "
190 P$(5)= "    /   \         ":
    P$(6)= "   /     \        "
200 P$(7)= "  |       |       ":
    P$(8)= "  ,       \       "
210 P$(9)= " | || || |        ":
    P$(10)="| || ||  \__,     "
220 P$(11)=" \_U-U_|__)       "
230 REM
240 REM DRAW FENCE
250 REM
260 FORJ=2TO9
270 PRINTCL$;
280 CO=5:X=0:Y=24:W=40:H=10:GOSUB810
290 CO=1:X=27:Y=15:W=13:H=16:GOSUB810
300 FORI=0TO24STEP3
310 CO=1:X=I:Y=14:W=2:H=13:GOSUB810
320 NEXT
330 CO=1:X=2:Y=4:W=27:H=1:GOSUB810:Y=12:
GOSUB810
340 PRINTHO$;:FORI=1TO5:PRINTCD$;:NEXT
350 FORI=1TO11:PRINTTAB(27);WH$;R1$;P$(I
):NEXT
```

```
360 W1=FNRN(J):W2=FNRN(J):IFW1=W2THENGOT
O360
370 T1$="TH":T2$="TH":IFW1=1THENT1$="ST"
380 T2$="TH":IFW2=1THENT2$="ST"
390 IFW1=2THENT1$="ND"
400 IFW2=2THENT2$="ND"
410 IFW1=3THENT1$="RD"
420 IFW2=3THENT2$="RD"
430 W1$=RIGHT$(STR$(W1),1):W2$=RIGHT$(ST
R$(W2),1)
440 PRINTHO$;:FORI=1TO16:PRINTCD$;:NEXT
450 PRINT"IS THE ";W1$;T1$;" NOTE IN THE
 TUNE HIGHER OR   LOWER THAN THE ";
460 PRINTW2$;T2$;" NOTE.":PRINT:PRINT"PR
ESS H OR L ";
470 N(0)=0
480 POKE54296,15:POKE54277,190:POKE54278
,248:POKE54276,17
490 FORK=1TOJ
500 REM
510 REM PLAY THE TUNE
520 REM
530 WN=FNRA(FNRN(14))
540 N(K)=VAL(MID$(N$,WN,2)):IFN(K)=N(K-1
)THENGOTO530
550 T(K)=VAL(MID$(N$,WN+2,3))
560 IFJ=2ANDN(1)=N(2)THENGOTO540
570 POKE54273,N(K):POKE54272,T(K):FORI=1
TO200:NEXT
580 FORI=1TO200:NEXTI
590 NEXTK
600 POKE54276,0:POKE54277,0:POKE54278,0
610 IFN(W1)>N(W2)THENA$="H"
620 IFN(W1)<N(W2)THENA$="L"
630 I=-3:I$="":ID=0
640 GETI$:IFI$=""ORID=1THENI=I+3:CO=2:X=
I:Y=14:W=2:H=13:GOSUB810
650 IFI<34AND(I$=""ORID=1)THENGOTO640
660 IFI$=A$ANDID=0THENPRINT:PRINT:PRINT"
YES,YOU ARE RIGHT":GOTO720
670 IFI<28THENPRINTI$;:ID=1:GOTO640
```

```
680 GOSUB940
690 POKE54276,0:POKE54277,0:POKE54278,0
700 IFA$="H"THENPRINT:PRINT:PRINT"NO,IT
IS HIGHER (H)"
710 IFA$="L"THENPRINT:PRINT:PRINT"NO IT
IS LOWER (L)"
720 PRINT:PRINT"HIT RETURN FOR MORE";:IN
PUTRB$
730 IFI$<>A$THENGOTO270
740 NEXTJ
750 PRINTCU$;S$
760 PRINTHO$;:FORI=1TO15:PRINTCD$;:NEXT
770 PRINT"A MUSICIAN LIKE YOURSELF SHOUL
D'NT   BE   PAINTING FENCES !           ";
780 PRINT"                ":FORI=1TO3:PRINTS
$;:NEXT
790 END
800 REM
810 REM BLOCK SUBROUTINE
820 FORX1=XTOX+W-1
830 FORY1=Y-H+1TOY
840 SD=(Y1*KL)+X1
850 POKECM+SD,CO
860 POKEPM+SD,160
870 NEXT
880 NEXT
890 RETURN
900 END
910 REM READ NOTES SUBROUTINE
920 N$="3407536085381264020043052451984 8
1275109754111571726112664188681497216 9"
930 RETURN
940 REM CAT GROWL SUBROUTINE
950 POKE54296,15:POKE54277,15 :POKE54276
,129:POKE54278,244
960 POKE54273,1:POKE54272,18:FORI=1TO300
970 NEXT:POKE54276,0:POKE54277,0:POKE542
78,0
980 RETURN
```

SEQUENCE COUNTDOWN

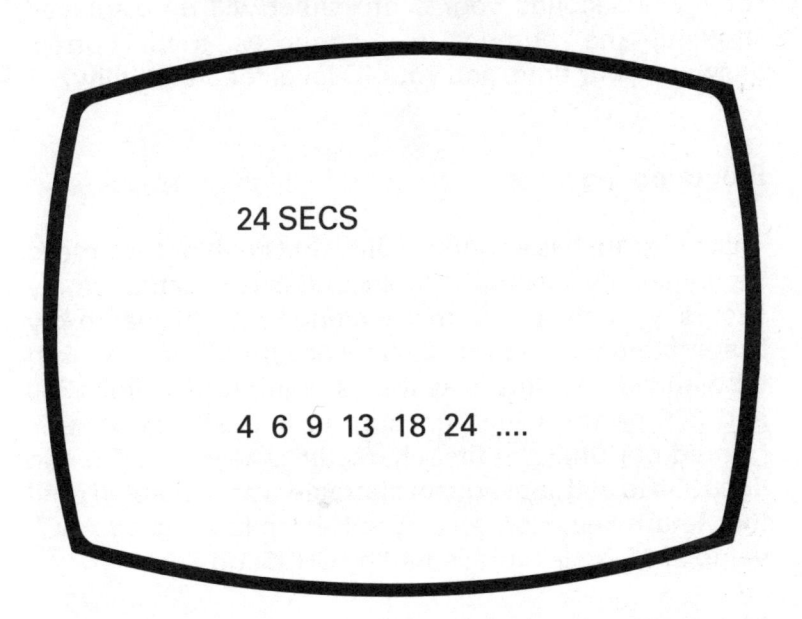

```
24 SECS




4 6 9 13 18 24 ....
```

Six numbers, or letters, will be displayed on the screen and it is up to you to provide the next logical item to complete the series.

How to play

When you have worked out your answer, type in your item and press RETURN.

If you cannot work out the correct answer, then move on as quickly as possible as you only have 200 seconds to complete as many answers as you can.

A wrong answer will bring you the correct result from your computer, and then you will be given the next sequence. If you wish to PASS on a question then press P and RETURN and you will be taken on to the next question.

After 200 seconds your score sheet will be displayed showing the number of sequences tried, correct answers, your time, and your IQ level for adaptibility.

Programming hints

This program has a useful facility that enables the time to be constantly displayed in seconds. This actually only occurs while the program is waiting for the player to key in something, but as most of any program's time is taken up with waiting, this is all that is required. The lines 330 and 360 perform this function. In line 330 the time is printed out until the first character is keyed in. Then in lines 350 to 360 subsequent characters are accepted until the Return key is pressed. The Return key has an ASCII value of 13, so is represented by CHR$(13).

One change you could make, is to add new sequences. To do this allow W to have a larger maximum value in line 170. The sequence must then be defined after line 210. The sequence is held in S(2), S(3), S(4), S(5), S(6), S(7) and S(8). S(2) is defined in line 150 and is fixed for all sequences. IC is another random value which may be useful when defining a sequence. The message saying how the sequence is created is held in MS$. If the last number in sequence S(8) is less than 26 then the sequence is converted to letters.

Program

```
10 REM SEQUENCE COUNTDOWN
20 REM COPYRIGHT (C) G.LUDINSKI 1983
30 CL$=CHR$(147):CG$=CHR$(151):HO$=CHR$(
19):RD$=CHR$(28)
```

```
40 POKE53280,2:POKE53281,12:PRINTCG$;CL$
;:REM BORDER AND BACKGROUND
50 DIMS(8)
60 POKE53272,23:REM LOWER CASE
70 TE=0:CR=0:TI$="000000"
80 PRINTCL$;
90 TE=TE+1
100 IFTE=11ORTI>=12000THENGOTO570
110 REM
120 REM WORK OUT SEQUENCE
130 REM
140 S(1)=0
150 S(2)=INT(RND(1)*9+1)
160 IC=INT(RND(1)*9+1)
170 W=INT(RND(1)*3)
180 FORI=3TO8
190 IFW=0THENS(I)=INT(2*S(I-1)-S(I-2)+IC
):GOSUB720
200 IFW=1THENS(I)=INT(S(I-1)+S(I-2)+IC):
GOSUB730
210 IFW=2THENS(I)=INT(S(2)↑(I-1)):GOSUB8
10
220 NEXTI
230 FORI=1TO13:PRINT:NEXTI
240 REM
250 REM DISPLAY SEQUENCE
260 REM
270 IFS(8)>26THENGOSUB680:XP=POS(0)
280 IFS(8)<=26THENGOSUB700:XP=POS(0)
290 REM
300 REM INPUT ANSWER
310 REM
320 IX=1
330 GETI$:IF I$=""THENPRINTHO$;INT(TI/60)
:GOTO330
340 VT=15:GOSUB740:PRINTTAB(XP-6);I$;
350 GET I2$: IF I2$ <> "" THEN I$=I$+I2$
360 IF I2$ <> "" AND I2$ <> CHR$(13) THE
N PRINTI2$;
370 IF I2$="" THEN GOTO 350
380 IF I2$=CHR$(13)THENI$=LEFT$(I$,LEN(I
$)-1):GOTO400
```

```
390 GOTO 350
400 REM
410 REM CHECK ANSWER
420 REM
430 GET RB$:IF RB$<>"" THEN GOTO 430
440 IFLE=0ANDABS(VAL(I$)-S(8))<=LEN(I$)/
2THENPRINTRD$;"  ⌐";:CR=CR+1:GOTO510
450 IF LE <> 1 THEN GOTO 470
460 IFI$=CHR$(64+S(8))ORI$=CHR$(65+S(8))
THENPRINTRD$;"  ⌐";:CR=CR+1:GOTO510
470 PRINT:PRINT:PRINT"/O,THE ANSWER =   "
;
480 IF LE=0THENPRINTS(8):GOTO500
490 PRINTCHR$(64+S(8)):PRINT:GOSUB790
500 PRINT:PRINTMS$
510 PRINTCG$;:PRINT:PRINT"⌐RESS RETURN T
O CONTINUE"
520 INPUTA$
530 GOTO80
540 REM
550 REM SCORE SHEET
560 REM
570 PRINTCL$;
580 PRINT"/UMBER OF SEQUENCES COMPLETED
 = ";TE
590 PRINT:PRINT"/UMBER CORRECT = ";CR
600 PRINT:PRINT"⌐IME TAKEN = ";INT(TI/60
);" SECONDS"
610 IQ=INT(CR*100/5.3)
620 PRINT:PRINT" ⌐OUR ⌐● LEVEL (ADAPTABIL
ITY) = ";IQ
630 PRINT
640 IFCR>=7THENPRINT"THIS IS CLASSED AS
SUPERIOR (UPPER 10%)":GOTO670
650 IFCR=6THENPRINT"THIS IS CLASSSD AS G
OOD (UPPER 20%)":GOTO670
660 IFCR=5THENPRINT"THIS IS CLASSED AS F
AIR (UPPER 60%)"
670 GOTO830
680 PRINTSTR$(S(2))" ";STR$(S(3));" ";ST
R$(S(4));" ";STR$(S(5));
```

```
690 PRINT" ";STR$(S(6));" ";STR$(S(7));"
......";:LE=0:RETURN
700 LE=1:PRINTCHR$(64+S(2));" ";CHR$(64+
S(3));" ";CHR$(64+S(4));
710 PRINT" ";CHR$(64+S(5));" ";CHR$(64+S
(6));" ";CHR$(64+S(7));" ......";:RETURN
720 MS$="THE INTERVAL INCREASES BY "+STR
$(IC)+" EACH TIME":RETURN
730 MS$="EACH NUMBER IS THE SUM OF THE P
REVIOUS  TWO PLUS "+STR$(IC):RETURN
740 PRINTHO$;
750 FOR GH=1 TO VT-2
760 PRINT
770 NEXT GH
780 RETURN
790 PRINT"REPLACE EACH LETTER BY ITS POS
ITION     NUMBER E.G 1 FOR A,2 FOR B ETC
."
800 RETURN
810 MS$="EACH NUMBER IS "+STR$(S(2))+" T
O THE POWER OF 1,2,3,4,5,6 AND 7"
820 RETURN
830 END
```

WHAT'S YOURS

Do you know that awful feeling when you have been put in charge of the drinks purchase at your friend's wedding?

You can be sure that you will get a soft drink for the big fellow in the corner or, even worse, a double whisky with pint chaser for someone's grandmother.

Anyway, it's your turn to buy the drinks and the order is on the bar. If you remember to get everyone the correct drink you will receive a whisky from each of them as they will be so pleased with your effort. If you get the **total** round correct, they will all pitch in and pay for the drinks themselves.

All the drinks are £1 each, so everytime you get the round right you make £1 per drink for yourself.

Oh, we almost forgot, everytime you get it right someone else joins your circle of friends.

How to play

Five different types of drinks can be ordered as follows:-

Beer	Brown Mug	B
Lager	Yellow Mug	L
Red Wine	Red Glass	R
White Wine	White Glass	W
Whisky	Yellow Glass	—

Look at the order detail on the bar and key in your copy. As you key in your order, the drinks will appear on the screen. When you finish the first round, a second will appear in a different order and, if the last round was correct, an additional member will be added to your group.

When the drink runs out, you can go home — by taxi.

Programming hints

This program is a good example of the use of user-defined graphics. Just two shapes are defined, a glass and a mug shape, but as they are displayed in many different colours there appears to be a large number of shapes. To create user-defined characters, move the character shapes from ROM to RAM, then redefine rarely-used characters such as hash and ampersand.

You may wish to add some more drinks in the appropriate shaped glass or mug. For example, a white beer mug could represent lemonade, or you could define a brandy or sherry glass shape. If you add more drinks you must allow W in line 410 to have a larger maximum value. Check for the letter that represents the new drinks in line 600. Display the new drinks after line 640.

Program

```
10 REM WHAT'S YOURS
20 REM COPYRIGHT (C) G.LUDINSKI 1983
30 POKE53280,3:POKE53281,12:POKE53272,21
:REM BORDER BACKGROUND AND UPPER CASE
40 DIMW(20)
50 HO$=CHR$(19):CL$=CHR$(147):CG$=CHR$(1
51):RD$=CHR$(28):WH$=CHR$(5)
60 CD$=CHR$(17):CU$=CHR$(145):BR$=CHR$(1
49):YE$=CHR$(158)
70 CM=55296:PM=1024:KL=40:REM COLOUR AND
 SCREEN MAP
80 S$="                    "
90 PRINTCL$;CG$;:FORI=1TO12:PRINTCD$;:NE
XT:PRINT"          PLEASE WAIT WHILE I THIN
K"
100 GOTO200
110 REM U.D.G. CALCULATOR SUBROUTINE
120 TF=0
130 FORL=0TO7
140 TF=TF+(2↑L)*VAL(MID$(N$,8-L,1))
150 NEXTL
160 RETURN
170 REM
180 REM DEFINE GLASS AND BEER MUG SHAPP
190 REM
200 Z$="0011111000011110001111100001110
0"
210 Z$=Z$+"0000100000001000000010000011
110
220 Y$="01111000011110001111100011110
10"
```

```
230 Y$=Y$+"01110100111101001111100 1111
000"
240 GOSUB850
250 MG$=CHR$(35):GL$=CHR$(38)
260 REM
270 REM DRAW BAR AND NOTE PADS
280 REM
290 PRINTCL$;
300 CO=9:X=0:Y=8:W=40:H=5:GOSUB780
310 CO=1:X=5:Y=24:W=10:H=10:GOSUB780
320 CO=1:X=25:Y=24:W=10:H=10:GOSUB780
330 PRINTHO$;:FORI=1TO16:PRINTCD$;:NEXT:
PRINTCG$;TAB(8);"BILL";TAB(28);"BACK"
340 PRINT:PRINTCG$;TAB(8);"£";TAB(28);"£
"
350 REM
360 REM DRAW DRINKS ORDERED
370 REM
380 M=0:OW=0
390 FORJ=2TO20
400 FORI=1TOJ
410 W(I)=INT(RND(1)*4)
420 IFW(I)=0THENCL=28:C$=GL$
430 IFW(I)=1THENCL=149:C$=MG$
440 IFW(I)=2THENCL=158:C$=MG$
450 IFW(I)=3THENCL=5:C$=GL$
460 PRINTHO$;:FORK=1TO3:PRINTCD$;:NEXT
470 PRINTCHR$(CL);TAB(I-1);C$;:POKECM+35
9+I,11:POKEPM+359+I,32
480 NEXTI
490 EI=0
500 PRINTHO$;:FORI=1TO11:PRINTCD$;:NEXT
510 PRINTCG$;"WHAT IS YOUR ORDER
              B=BEER   L=LAGER R=RED WINE
";
520 PRINT" W=WHITE WINE"
530 OW=OW+J
540 REM
550 REM DRAW DRINKS BOUGHT
560 REM
570 FORK=1TOJ
580 GETI$:IFI$=""THENGOTO580
```

```
590 IFK=1THENPRINTHO$;CD$;CD$;CD$;LEFT$(
S$,20):PRINTCU$;CU$
600 IFI$<>"B"ANDI$<>"L"ANDI$<>"R"ANDI$<>
"W"THENGOTO580
610 IFI$="R"THENPRINTRD$;TAB(K-1);GL$;:I
P=0
620 IFI$="W"THENPRINTWH$;TAB(K-1);GL$;:I
P=3
630 IFI$="B"THENPRINTBR$;TAB(K-1);MG$;:I
P=1
640 IFI$="L"THENPRINTYE$;TAB(K-1);MG$;:I
P=2
650 IFIP=W(K)THENPOKECM+359+K,7:POKEPM+3
59+K,38:M=M+1:GOTO670
660 EI=1
670 P$=STR$(OW):XT=9:YT=18:GOSUB1210:P$=
STR$(M):XT=29:GOSUB1210
680 NEXTK
690 IFEI=0THENM=M+J:P$=STR$(M):XT=29:YT=
18:GOSUB1210
700 FORI=1TO1000:GETRB$:NEXTI
710 IFEI=1THENGOTO400
720 NEXTJ
730 PRINTHO$;:FORI=1TO11:PRINTCD$;:NEXT
740 PRINTCG$;"YOU DID IT ! YOU WILL NEED
 A REAL DRINK AFTER THAT";LEFT$(S$,29)
750 GOTO1290
760 REM
770 REM BLOCK SUBROUTINE
780 FORY1=Y-H+1TOY
790 FORX1=XTOX+W-1
800 SD=(Y1*KL)+X1
810 POKECM+SD,CO
820 POKEPM+SD,27
830 NEXT:NEXT
840 RETURN
850 REM DEFINE GLASS AND MUG SHAPE SUBRO
UTINE
860 POKE56334,PEEK(56334)AND254:POKE1,PE
EK(1)AND251
870 C1=12288:C0=53248
880 FORI=0TO63
```

```
890 FORJ=0TO7
900 POKEC1+I*8+J,PEEK(C0+I*8+J)
910 NEXT
920 NEXT
930 POKE1,PEEK(1)OR4:POKE56334,PEEK(5633
4)OR1
940 POKE53272,(PEEK(53272)AND240)+12
950 REM
960 REM REDEFINE CHR. 35 AS A MUG
970 REM
980 CG=12568
990 FORI=0TO7
1000 N$=MID$(Y$,I*8+1,8)
1010 GOSUB110
1020 POKECG+I,TF
1030 NEXT
1040 REM
1050 REM REDEFINE CHR. 38 AS A GLASS
1060 REM
1070 CG=12592
1080 FORI=0TO7
1090 N$=MID$(Z$,I*8+1,8)
1100 GOSUB110
1110 POKECG+I,TF
1120 NEXT
1130 REM
1140 REM REDEFINE CHR. 27 AS A BLOCK
1150 REM
1160 CG=12504
1170 FORI=0TO7
1180 POKECG+I,255
1190 NEXT
1200 RETURN
1210 REM POKE SCREEN SUBROUTINE
1220 FORFF=XTTOXT+LEN(P$)-1
1230 SD=(KL*YT)+FF
1240 POKECM+SD,11
1250 CC$=MID$(P$,FF-XT+1,1)
1260 POKEPM+SD,ASC(CC$)
1270 NEXT
1280 RETURN
1290 END
```

PATTERN PAIRS

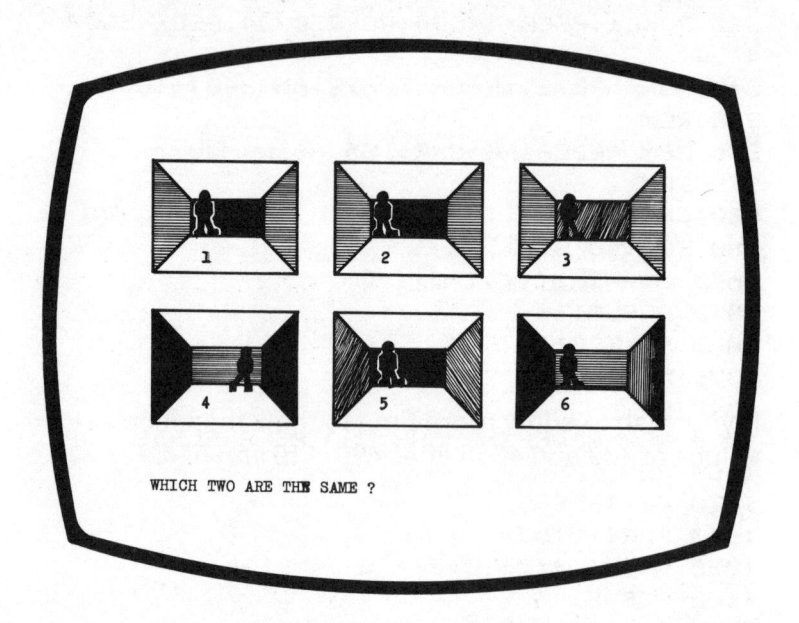

WHICH TWO ARE THE SAME ?

If you have tried Odd One Out in this book, then you will find this following puzzle a little more difficult.

There are six pictures displayed on the screen, in a range of colours, and you have only a few seconds to compare them and nominate the pair, you believe, are a match.

How to play

Identify your pair, note the numbers alongside and key in your answer. You don't have to key in your answer in strict chronological order. Just punch in your numbers and wait. Correct responses will be rewarded with a pleasant little high pitched tune, but wrong answers will be faced with a low pitched little dirge.

To continue, press Y for Yes and to stop, press N for No, remembering to press RETURN after your response.

A score sheet will appear if you press N showing your tries, results, time and average time.

Programming hints

Each of the pictures is slightly different except for the matching pair. This is done by adding HX and HY to the position of the man in the picture subroutine and HX and HY will be different for each picture except the two that are the same. The same applies to the room colours.

If you wish to allow more time to think then increase the values of 100 and 40 in lines 490, 510 and 520.

Program

```
10 REM PATTERN PAIRS
20 REM COPYRIGHT (C) G.LUDINSKI 1983
30 DIMP$(6),CO$(7)
40 POKE53280,2:POKE53281,12:POKE53272,21
:REM BORDER BACKGROUND AND UPPER CASE
50 S1=54273:S2=54272:REM SOUND VARIABLES
60 HO$=CHR$(19):CL$=CHR$(147):CG$=CHR$(1
51):CU$=CHR$(145):CD$=CHR$(17)
70 R1$=CHR$(18):R0$=CHR$(146)
80 CO$(1)=CHR$(30):CO$(2)=CHR$(31):CO$(3
)=CHR$(129):CO$(4)=CHR$(149)
90 CO$(5)=CHR$(156):CO$(6)=CHR$(158):CO$
(7)=CHR$(159)
100 V=53248:POKEV+21,63:REM ENABLE SPRIT
ES
110 FORK=0TO5:POKE2040+K,13:NEXT:REM SPR
ITE DATA AREA
120 GOSUB950
130 NU=0:CR=0
140 TI$="000000"
150 P$(1)="54444444446"
160 P$(2)="15          69"
```

```
170 P$(3)="11333333399"
180 P$(4)="11333333399"
190 P$(5)="17        89"
200 P$(6)="72A22222228"
210 PRINTCL$;CG$;
220 NU=NU+1
230 PT=0:PC=0
240 PRINT
250 REM
260 REM GENERATE PICTURES
270 REM
280 W1=INT(RND(1)*6+1)
290 W2=INT(RND(1)*6+1):IFW2=W1THENGOTO290
300 W$=RIGHT$(STR$(W1),1)+RIGHT$(STR$(W2),1)
310 W1$=RIGHT$(STR$(W2),1)+RIGHT$(STR$(W1),1)
320 CI=INT(RND(1)*4+1)
330 XI=INT(RND(1)*35+24)
340 YI=INT(RND(1)*8+50)
350 REM
360 REM DRAW PICTURES
370 REM
380 FORYD=10TO66STEP56
390 FORXD=0TO208STEP104
400 GOSUB750
410 NEXTXD
420 NEXTYD
430 REM
440 REM QUESTION
450 REM
460 PRINTHO$:FORK=1TO15:PRINTCD$;:NEXT
470 PRINTCG$;"WHICH TWO ARE THE SAME ";
480 I1$="":I2$="":I=0:IC=0
490 GETI1$:IFI1$=""ANDI<100THENI=I+1:GOTO490
500 PRINTI1$;
510 GETI2$:IFI2$=""ANDIC<40THENIC=IC+1:GOTO510
520 IFI=100ORIC=40THENPRINT:GOTO570
530 IFI$<>""AND(I$<"1"ORI$>"6")THENGOTO490
```

```
540 PRINTI2$
550 I$=I1$+I2$
560 IFI$=W$ORI$=W1$THENPRINT:PRINT"YES,Y
OU ARE RIGHT":GOSUB1280:CR=CR+1:GOTO580
570 PRINT:PRINT"NO,";W1;" AND";W2;" ARE
THE SAME":GOSUB1330
580 PRINT:PRINT"DO YOU WANT MORE Y/N";
590 INPUTR$
600 IFR$<>"N"THENGOTO210
610 REM
620 REM SCORE SHEET
630 REM
640 PRINTCL$;
650 FORS=0TO5:POKEV+39+S,12:NEXTS
660 PRINT:PRINTTAB(13);"PATTERN PAIRS"
670 FORI=1TO9:PRINT:NEXTI
680 PRINT:PRINT"PROBLEMS COMPLETED =";NU
690 TM=INT(TI/60)
700 PRINT:PRINT"PROBLEMS CORRECT = ";CR
710 PRINT:PRINT"TIME TAKEN = ";TM;" SECS
"
720 IFCR<>0THENPRINT:PRINT"TIME PER CORR
ECT PROBLEM = ";INT(TM/CR);" SECS"
730 GOTO1590
740 REM
750 REM PICTURE SUBROUTINE
760 PT=PT+1
770 IFPT=1THENMX=0
780 HX=0:HY=0
790 IFPT=VAL(RIGHT$(W$,1))ORPT=VAL(LEFT$
(W$,1))THENHX=40:HY=12:GOTO810
800 PC=PC+1:HX=PC*9:HY=PC*3
810 X=XI+XD+HX:IFXI+HX>100THENGOTO810
820 Y=YI+YD+HY:IFYI+HY>70THENGOTO820
830 CL=0
840 POKEV+38+PT,CL
850 IFX>=255THENMX=MX+2↑(PT-1):X=X-255
860 POKEV+2*(PT-1),X:POKEV+16,MX
870 POKEV+(2*PT)-1,Y
880 PRINTHO$:IFPT>3THENFORK=1TO7:PRINTCD
$;:NEXT
890 FORZ=1TO6
900 IFPT<4THENPRINTTAB(13*(PT-1));:GOTO9
20
```

```
910 PRINTTAB(13*(PT-4));
920 P$=P$(Z):GOSUB1390:NEXT
930 RETURN
940 REM END
950 REM READ SPRITE SHAPE SUBROUTINE
960 RESTORE
970 FORS=0TO62
980 READ SP
990 POKE832+S,SP
1000 NEXT
1010 GOTO 1230
1020 DATA 0,24,0
1030 DATA 0,60,0
1040 DATA 0,60,0
1050 DATA 0,60,0
1060 DATA 0,28,0
1070 DATA 0,8,0
1080 DATA 0,28,0
1090 DATA 0,60,0
1100 DATA 0,124,0
1110 DATA 0,254,0
1120 DATA 1,191,0
1130 DATA 3,61,0
1140 DATA 0,60,128
1150 DATA 0,60,0
1160 DATA 0,60,0
1170 DATA 0,60,0
1180 DATA 0,108,0
1190 DATA 0,102,0
1200 DATA 0,67,0
1210 DATA 1,193,128
1220 DATA 0,195,0
1230 RETURN
1240 REM SOUND ON SUBROUTINE
1250 POKE54296,15:POKE54277,190:POKE54270,248:POKE54276,33:RETURN
1260 REM SOUND OFF SUBROUTINE
1270 POKE54276,0:POKE54277,0:POKE54278,0:RETURN
1280 REM RIGHT-SOUND SUBROUTINE
1290 GOSUB1240
1300 POKES1,68:POKES2,149:FORTT=1TO200:NEXTTT
```

```
1310 GOSUB1260
1320 RETURN
1330 REM WRONG-SOUND SUBROUTINE
1340 GOSUB1240
1350 POKES1,45:POKES2,198:FORTT=1TO200:N
EXTTT
1360 POKES1,43:POKES2,52:FORTT=1TO100:NE
XTTT
1370 GOSUB1260
1380 RETURN
1390 REM DISPLAY ROOM SUBROUTINE
1400 C1$=CO$(PC):C2$=CO$(PC+1):C3$=CO$(P
C+2)
1410 IFPT<>VAL(RIGHT$(W$,1))ANDPT<>VAL(L
EFT$(W$,1))THENGOTO1430
1420 C1$=CO$(CI+1):C2$=CO$(CI):C3$=CO$(C
I+2)
1430 FORQ=1TO11
1440 C$=MID$(P$,Q,1)
1450 IFC$=" "THENPRINTCG$;" ";:GOTO1560
1460 IFC$="1"THENPRINTC1$;R1$;" ";R0$;:G
OTO1560
1470 IFC$="2"THENPRINTCG$;CHR$(164);:GOT
O1560
1480 IFC$="3"THENPRINTC2$;R1$;" ";R0$;:G
OTO1560
1490 IFC$="4"THENPRINTCG$;CHR$(163);:GOT
O1560
1500 IFC$="5"THENPRINTC1$;R1$;CHR$(127);
R0$;:GOTO1560
1510 IFC$="6"THENPRINTC3$;R1$;CHR$(169);
R0$;:GOTO1560
1520 IFC$="7"THENPRINTC1$;CHR$(169);:GOT
O1560
1530 IFC$="8"THENPRINTC3$;CHR$(127);:GOT
O1560
1540 IFC$="9"THENPRINTC3$;R1$;" ";R0$;:G
OTO1560
1550 PRINTRIGHT$(STR$(PT),1);
1560 NEXT
1570 PRINT
1580 RETURN
1590 END
```

CONCENTRATION TEST

This time we have given a little longer to work out your answers, because we think you'll need all the brainpower at your command.

On the screen will be displayed 19 rows of 35 numbers and you have eight minutes to find as many pairs of adjacent numbers, whose sum is 10, as possible.

These pairs must be in the same row.

How to play

When you have found the matching pairs, key in the row number followed by the column number of each, and then press RETURN Example A3, A4. Always place a comma between each entry. If your pair of numbers is correct they will be rubbed out.

You may key in the pairs in any order and, if you cannot find any 'missing' pairs before your time is up, type in NO, MORE followed by RETURN. Again, there must be a comma between the words.

This ending of the game will cause your score sheet to be displayed. If you fail to complete in the alloted time the score sheet will automatically appear.

Your score sheet will give a classification and an IQ rating on your powers of concentration.

Programming hints

Lines 150-240 draw out the matrix of numbers and the row and column labels. Note that the letters are displayed in a loop by referring to their ASCII values. As the letter A has ASCII value of 65, B has a value of 66 etc so CHR$(64+J) where J is 1,2,3 etc. will display the letters A,B,C etc.

I would not advise any alterations as the scoring and IQ levels were determined by scientific testing, and any changes would make the scores and IQ level incorrect.

Program
```
10 REM CONCENTRATION TESTER
20 REM COPYRIGHT (C) G.LUDINSKI 1983
30 HO$=CHR$(19):CL$=CHR$(147):CG$=CHR$(1
51):R1$=CHR$(18):R0$=CHR$(146)
40 CU$=CHR$(145):R1=0
50 POKE53280,2:POKE53281,12:POKE53272,23
60 PRINTCG$;
70 DIMA$(35,23)
80 PRINTCL$;
90 NU=0
```

```
100 TI$="000000"
110 ER=0
120 REM
130 REM DRAW MATRIX
140 REM
150 PRINT"            1                   2
 3"
160 PRINT"   123456789012345678901234566 8
9012345"
170 FORJ=1TO19
180 PRINT:PRINTCHR$(64+J);" ";
190 FORI=1TO35
200 A$(I,J)=STR$(INT(RND(1)*10))
210 PRINTRIGHT$(A$(I,J),1);
220 NEXTI
230 PRINT" ";CHR$(64+J);
240 NEXTJ
250 REM
260 REM QUESTION
270 REM
280 PRINT
290 PRINTHO$;:FORG=1TO22:PRINT:NEXT:PRIN
T"|YPE ROW COL. COMMA ROW COL. SO X+Y=10
 ";
300 PRINT:INPUTC$,D$
310 REM
320 REM CHECK INPUT
330 REM
340 IFTI>=28800THENGOTO520
350 IFC$="NO"ANDD$="MORE"THENGOTO520
360 IFLEN(C$)<2ORLEN(D$)<2THENGOSUB730:G
OTO300
370 J=ASC(LEFT$(C$,1))-64
380 I=VAL(MID$(C$,2,LEN(C$)-1))
390 K=ASC(LEFT$(D$,1))-64
400 L=VAL(MID$(D$,2,LEN(D$)-1))
410 IFI<10ORI>35ORJ<10RJ>23ORL<10RL>35ORK
<10RK>22THENGOSUB730:GOTO300
420 IFJ<>KTHENGOSUB730:GOTO300
430 IFVAL(A$(I,J))+VAL(A$(L,K))<>10THENE
R=ER+1:GOSUB730:GOTO300
440 P$=" ":HT=I+1:VT=J+2:GOSUB790
```

```
450 P$=" ":HT=L+1:VT=K+2:GOSUB790
460 VT=23:P$=" ":FORHT=0TO30:GOSUB790:NE
XT
470 NU=NU+1
480 P$="              ":VT=30:GOSUB780:PRINTCU
$;CU$;CU$;CU$;:GOTO290
490 REM
500 REM SCORE SHEET
510 REM
520 PRINTCL$;:PRINT:PRINT:PRINT" |OU FOUN
D ";NU;" PAIRS"
530 MAX=0
540 FORJ=1TO19
550 FORI=1TO34
560 IFVAL(A$(I,J))+VAL(A$(I+1,J))=10THEN
MAX=MAX+1
570 NEXTI
580 NEXTJ
590 SC=MAX-NU+ER
600 PRINT:PRINT" |OUR SCORE IS ";SC:PRINT
610 AV=MAX*0.6:IQ=INT((NU/AV)*100)
620 IFIQ>150THENIQ=150
630 IFSC<0.6*SCTHENPRINT" |OU ARE CLASSED
 AS SUPERIOR (UPPER 10%)":GOTO660
640 IFSC<0.9*SCTHENPRINT" |OU ARE CLASSED
 AS GOOD (UPPER 30%)":GOTO50
650 IFSC<1.1*SCTHENPRINT" |OU ARE CLASSED
 AS FAIR (UPPER 60%)"
660 PRINT:PRINT" |OUR ╮● LEVEL (CONCENTRA
TION) = ";IQ
670 PRINT:PRINT"─O YOU WANT MORE (Y/N)"
680 INPUTI$
690 IFI$<>"Y"ANDI$<>"N"THENPRINTCU$;:GOT
O680
700 IFI$="Y"THENGOTO80
710 GOTO770
720 REM
730 REM ERROR
740 REM
750 PRINTCU$;CU$;:PRINT"─RROR:TYPE ROW,C
OL. COMMA ROW COL.SO=10";
```

```
760 RETURN
770 END
780 HT=0
790 VV=1024+(VT*40)
800 POKE VV + HT,ASC(P$)+R1*128
810 RETURN
```

ODD ONE OUT

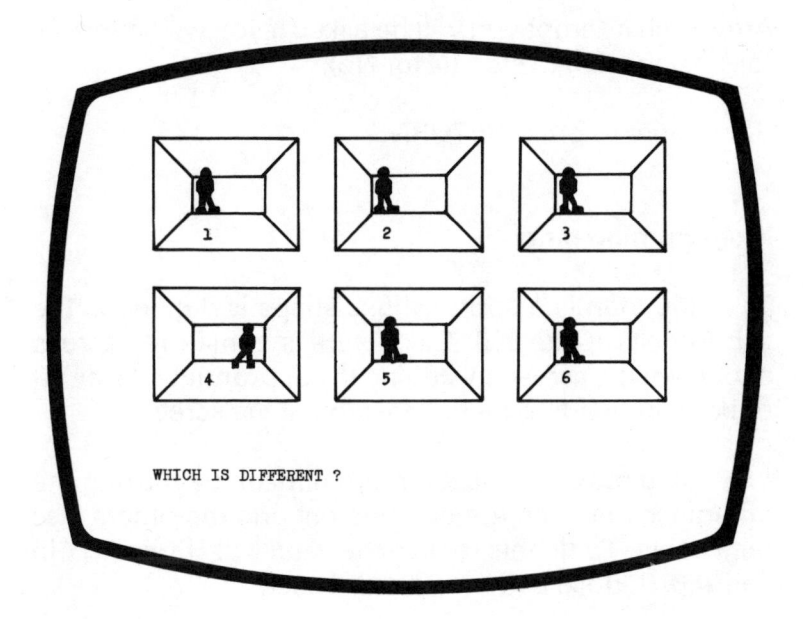

WHICH IS DIFFERENT ?

Six pictures are displayed on the screen and you are given only a few seconds to compare them and identify the odd one out.

A score sheet will be displayed, showing the number of puzzles completed, number correct and the time and average time taken.

How to play

Each of the pictures on the screen will be identified by a number, and you must key in the appropriate number as your guess.

If you get the answer wrong, you will be told the correct

answer, to the accompaniment of a rather low pitched little tune. Get it right, however, and you will hear a pleasant little tune.

After each attempt you will be asked if you wish more (Y for Yes) or wish to stop (N for No).

Remember to press RETURN.

Programming hints

The little man is a sprite whose shape is defined in the subroutine on line 850. The picture is transferred across and down the screen by adding the appropriate XD or YD or both, depending on the position of the screen.

You could make the puzzle more difficult by making the difference between the odd one out and the others less noticeable. To do this reduce the values of HX and HY in line 760. Reduce both numbers of each.

Program

```
10 REM ODD ONE OUT
20 REM COPYRIGHT (C) G.LUDINSKI 1983
30 POKE53280,2:POKE53281,12:POKE53272,21
:REM BORDER BACKGROUND AND UPPER CASE
40 S1=54273:S2=54272:REM SOUND VARIABLES
50 HO$=CHR$(19):CL$=CHR$(147):CG$=CHR$(1
51):CU$=CHR$(145):CD$=CHR$(17)
60 V=53248:POKEV+21,63:REM ENABLE SPRITE
S
70 FORK=0TO5:POKE2040+K,13:NEXT:REM SPRI
TE DATA AREA
80 GOSUB850
90 NU=0:CR=0
100 TI$="000000"
110 PRINTCL$;CG$;
120 NU=NU+1
```

```
130 PT=0
140 REM
150 REM DRAW FRAMEWORK
160 REM
170 PRINT
180 FORK=1TO2
190 P$="1544444444463154444444446315444
4444403":GOSUB1290
200 P$="1 5       6 31 5       6 31 5
    6 3":GOSUB1290
210 P$="1 144444443 31 144444443 31 1444
44443 3":GOSUB1290
220 P$="1 122222223 31 122222223 31 1222
22223 3":GOSUB1290
230 P$="1 6       5 31 6       5 31 6
    5 3":GOSUB1290
240 IFK=1THENP$="162A222222253162B222222
253162C222222253":GOSUB1290
250 IFK=2THENP$="162D222222253162E222222
253162F222222253":GOSUB1290
260 PRINT
270 NEXT
280 REM
290 REM GENERATE SHAPES
300 REM
310 W=INT(RND(1)*6+1)
320 CL=INT(RND(1)*3)
330 XI=INT(RND(1)*40+24)
340 YI=INT(RND(1)*10+50)
350 REM
360 REM DRAW PATTERNS
370 REM
380 FORYD=10TO66STEP56
390 FORXD=0TO210STEP105
400 GOSUB720
410 NEXTXD
420 NEXTYD
430 REM
440 REM QUESTION
450 REM
460 PRINTHO$:FORK=1TO15:PRINTCD$;:NEXT
470 PRINT"WHICH IS DIFFERENT ";
```

```
480 I$="":I=0
490 GETI$:IFI$=""ANDI<80THENI=I+1:GOTO490
500 IFI=80THENPRINT:GOTO540
510 IFI$<>""AND(I$<"1"ORI$>"6")THENGOTO490
520 PRINTI$
530 IFVAL(I$)=WTHENPRINT:PRINT"YES,YOU ARE RIGHT":GOSUB1180:CR=CR+1:GOTO550
540 PRINT:PRINT"NO, ";W;" IS DIFFERENT":GOSUB1230
550 PRINT:PRINT"DO YOU WANT MORE Y/N";
560 INPUTR$
570 IFR$<>"N"THENGOTO110
580 REM
590 REM SCORE SHEET
600 REM
610 PRINTCL$;
620 FORS=0TO5:POKEV+39+S,12:NEXTS
630 PRINT:PRINTTAB(14);"ODD ONE OUT"
640 FORI=1TO9:PRINT:NEXTI
650 PRINT:PRINT"PROBLEMS COMPLETED =";NU
660 TM=INT(TI/60)
670 PRINT:PRINT"PROBLEMS CORRECT = ";CR
680 PRINT:PRINT"TIME TAKEN = ";TM;" SECS"
690 IFCR<>0THENPRINT:PRINT"TIME PER CORRECT PROBLEM = ";INT(TM/CR);" SECS"
700 GOTO1430
710 REM
720 REM PATTERN SUBROUTINE
730 PT=PT+1
740 IFPT=1THENMX=0
750 HX=0:HY=0
760 IFPT=WTHENHX=INT(RND(1)*20+20):HY=INT(RND(1)*5+5)
770 X=XI+XD+HX:IFXI+HX>100THENGOTO770
780 Y=YI+YD+HY:IFYI+HY>70THENGOTO780
790 POKEV+38+PT,CL
800 IFX>=255THENMX=MX+2↑(PT-1):X=X-255
810 POKEV+2*(PT-1),X:POKEV+16,MX
820 POKEV+(2*PT)-1,Y
```

```
830 RETURN
840 REM END
850 REM READ SPRITE SHAPE SUBROUTINE
860 RESTORE
870 FORS=0TO62
880 READ SP
890 POKE832+S,SP
900 NEXT
910 GOTO 1130
920 DATA 0,24,0
930 DATA 0,60,0
940 DATA 0,60,0
950 DATA 0,60,0
960 DATA 0,28,0
970 DATA 0,8,0
980 DATA 0,28,0
990 DATA 0,60,0
1000 DATA 0,124,0
1010 DATA 0,254,0
1020 DATA 1,191,0
1030 DATA 3,61,0
1040 DATA 0,60,128
1050 DATA 0,60,0
1060 DATA 0,60,0
1070 DATA 0,60,0
1080 DATA 0,108,0
1090 DATA 0,102,0
1100 DATA 0,67,0
1110 DATA 1,193,128
1120 DATA 0,195,0
1130 RETURN
1140 REM SOUND ON SUBROUTINE
1150 POKE54296,15:POKE54277,190:POKE54270,248:POKE54276,33:RETURN
1160 REM SOUND OFF SUBROUTINE
1170 POKE54276,0:POKE54277,0:POKE54278,0:RETURN
1180 REM RIGHT-SOUND SUBROUTINE
1190 GOSUB1140
1200 POKES1,68:POKES2,149:FORTT=1TO200:NEXTTT
```

```
1210 GOSUB1160
1220 RETURN
1230 REM WRONG-SOUND SUBROUTINE
1240 GOSUB1140
1250 POKES1,45:POKES2,198:FORTT=1TO200:N
EXTTT
1260 POKES1,43:POKES2,52:FORTT=1TO100:NE
XTTT
1270 GOSUB1160
1280 RETURN
1290 REM PRINT PET CHARACTERS SUBROUTINE
1300 FORQ=1TO39
1310 C$=MID$(P$,Q,1)
1320 IFC$=" "THENPRINT" ";:GOTO1400
1330 IFC$="1"THENPRINTCHR$(167);:GOTO140
0
1340 IFC$="2"THENPRINTCHR$(164);:GOTO140
0
1350 IFC$="3"THENPRINTCHR$(165);:GOTO140
0
1360 IFC$="4"THENPRINTCHR$(163);:GOTO140
0
1370 IFC$="5"THENPRINTCHR$(109);:GOTO140
0
1380 IFC$="6"THENPRINTCHR$(110);:GOTO140
0
1390 PRINTCHR$(ASC(C$)-16);
1400 NEXT
1410 PRINT
1420 RETURN
1430 END
```

DECISIVE HERO

```
            ☒ ☒
         ▄▄ ▄▄ ▄▄
    ────────────────────── ● ──

        A ldershot    1 8 5
        B racknell    5 2 2
        C amberley    7 3 5
        D orking      3 5 6
        E gham        3 2 1
        F arnham      2 8 2
        G uildford    5 7 7
        H enley       1 8 7
```

The wicked Baron has captured your love, Loretta, and tied her to the railroad track. Only you can save her from a grisly fate, but you will have to think fast and act even quicker. Wherever the Baron has taken her, you can be sure that it will be in a town far away from you, and you must work out the three possibilities, key in your answers and stop the train.

Please act quickly, as the thought of losing Loretta is too terrible to contemplate.

How to play

The names of eight towns will be displayed on the screen with letters A to H. Against each of the letters you will be shown a combination of numbers.

You must decide which three series of numbers are the highest, type them in and stop the train.

Example: from the screen shown above you will see that the correct answer is C, G and H. You don't have to key in your answers in alphabetical order, just key them in correctly and quickly. If you stop the train or, unfortunately for Loretta, the train reaches the end of the screen, you will be asked if you wish to continue or end the program.

Press C and RETURN to continue, or E and RETURN to end the game.

Skill rating

When the game ends, a score sheet will be displayed showing your total, giving a qualitative rating and an IQ level of your decisiveness. This is not a true IQ level as intelligence is made up of reasoning ability, memory etc. but this result will be an indication of your IQ decisiveness level.

Classifications below Fair are omitted, as I know that if you are using this book you are above average!

Programming hints

This program defines two different shape sprites. A train shape which is sprite zero and takes its shape from area 13, and a smoke shape which is sprite one and takes its shape from area 192.

If you wish to increase the time for the engine to reach Loretta then increase the 4 in line 1090 to allow the smoke to travel further before the train moves. Also increase the maximum value of I in line 270 to the same number to ensure that these new smoke positions are defined. Ensure that the DIMensions of arrays X and Y are also increased to this value in line 40.

The program contains lower case letter Ls. Make sure you do not confuse them with ones.

Program

```
10 REM DECISIVE HERO
20 REM COPYRIGHT (C) G.LUDINSKI 1983
30 POKE53280,2:POKE53281,12:POKE53272,23
:REM BORDER BACKGROUND AND LOWER CASE
40 DIMA$(3),X(12),Y(12),N(3,8),S(8),T$(8
),TW(8)
50 HO$=CHR$(19):CL$=CHR$(147):CG$=CHR$(1
51):CU$=CHR$(145):CD$=CHR$(17)
60 RL$=CHR$(184):YE$=CHR$(158)
70 PRINTCL$;CG$;
80 S$="                                  "
90 S1=54273:S2=54272:VL=54296:WV=54276:A
D=54277:SR=54278:REM SOUND VARIABLES
100 REM
110 REM SPRITE 0 AND 1 ENABLE AND DATA A
REA
120 REM
130 V=53248:POKEV+21,3
140 POKE2040,13:POKE2041,192
150 REM
160 REM STORE TOWN NAMES
170 REM
180 RESTORE:FORI=1TO8:READT$(I):NEXTI
190 GOSUB1320
200 REM
210 REM STORE POSITIONS OF SMOKE
220 REM
```

```
230 FORI=1TO2
240 X(I)=64-I*8
250 Y(I)=16-I*8
260 NEXTI
270 FORI=3TO12
280 Y(I)=16
290 X(I)=72-I*8
300 NEXTI
310 TE=0:ER=0:CR=0
320 REM
330 REM THE ACTION STARTS HERE
340 REM
350 PRINTCL$;CG$;
360 TE=TE+1:MX=0
370 REM
380 REM STORE LISTS OF NUMBERS AND THEIR SUMS
390 REM
400 FORK=1TO7:S(K)=0:NEXTK
410 FORJ=1TO8
420 FORI=1TO3
430 N(I,J)=INT(RND(1)*9+1)
440 S(J)=S(J)+N(I,J)
450 NEXTI
460 NEXTJ
470 FORI=1TO8:TW(I)=I:NEXTI
480 REM
490 REM  BUBBLE SORT OF THE SUMS OF EACH LIST
500 REM
510 FORJ=1TO6
520 FORI=1TO7
530 IFS(I) >= S(I+1) THENGOTO550
540 TP=S(I):S(I)=S(I+1):S(I+1)=TP:TP=TW(I):TW(I)=TW(I+1):TW(I+1)=TP
550 NEXTI
560 NEXTJ
570 REM
580 REM CHECK FOR ANY DUPLICATES
590 REM
600 TWN=3:FORI=4TO8
```

```
610 IFS(I)=S(1)ORS(I)=S(2)ORS(I)=S(3)THE
NTWN=I
620 NEXTI
630 REM
640 REM DISPLAY PROBLEM
650 REM
660 PRINT:PRINT:PRINT:PRINT:PRINT:PRINT
670 FORZ=1TO31:PRINTRL$;:NEXT:PRINTYE$;"
O";CG$;RL$;RL$;RL$;RL$;RL$;RL$
680 PRINT:PRINT:PRINT
690 FORJ=1TO8
700 PRINTLEFT$(S$,10);LEFT$(T$(J),1);" "
;RIGHT$(T$(J),9);"    ";
710 FORI=1TO3
720 PRINTSTR$(N(I,J));" ";
730 NEXTI
740 PRINT
750 NEXTJ
760 PRINT
770 C1=0
780 GOSUB940
790 GOSUB1800
800 POKE198,0
810 PRINTHO$;:FORK=1TO22:PRINTCD$;:NEXT
820 PRINT"7RESS - TO CONTINUE OR - TO EN
D PROGRAM":INPUTC$
830 IFC$="C"ORC$="-"THENGOTO350
840 GOSUB1140
850 GOTO1860
860 REM
870 REM SMOKE SUBROUTINE
880 POKEV+40,1:REM COLOUR
890 X=24+X(I)+L*8:Y=Y(I)+50
900 IFX>=255THENMX=MX+2:X=X-255
910 POKEV+2,X:POKEV+16,MX
920 POKEV+3,Y
930 RETURN
940 REM TRAIN SUBROUTINE
950 POKEV+39,6:REM COLOUR
960 FORL=1TO22
970 GETI$
980 IFI$=""THENGOTO1030
```

```
990 FORJ=1TOTWN
1000 IFI$=CHR$(64+TW(J))THENC1=C1+1:GOSU
B1700:GOTO1030
1010 NEXTJ
1020 ER=ER+1
1030 IFC1=3THENCR=CR+1:GOTO1130
1040 X=74+L*8:Y=74
1050 IFX>=255THENMX=MX+1:X=X-255
1060 POKEV,X:POKEV+16,MX
1070 POKEV+1,Y
1080 GOSUB1750
1090 FORI=1TO4
1100 GOSUB870
1110 NEXT
1120 NEXTL
1130 RETURN
1140 REM IQ SUBROUTINE
1150 PRINTCL$;CG$;
1160 FORK=1TO7:PRINTCD$;:NEXT
1170 PRINT:PRINT"/UMBER OF TESTS COMPLET
ED = ";TE
1180 PRINT:PRINT"/UMBER OF TESTS CORRECT
 = ";CR
1190 PRINT:PRINT"/UMBER OF INCORRECT ANS
WERS = ";ER
1200 SC=INT(((ER*3)+((TE-CR)*10))/TE)
1210 PRINT
1220 IFSC<5THENPRINT"|HIS IS CLASSED AS
♥⌐┬─┐┌─ (UPPER 10%)":GOTO1250
1230 IFSC<7THENPRINT"|HIS IS CLASSED AS
|┌┬─ (UPPER 30%)":GOTO1250
1240 IFSC<9THENPRINT"|HIS IS CLASSED AS
─♠⌐─ (UPPER 60%)"
1250 IFSC=0THENIQU=150:GOTO1270
1260 IQU=INT(760/SC):IFIQU>150THENQU=150
1270 PRINT:PRINT" |OUR ⌐.■. LEVEL (DECISI
VENESS) = "; IQU
1280 RETURN
1290 DATA "♠LDERSHOT ","|RACKNELL ","─AM
BERLEY ","─ORKING   ","─GHAM     "
1300 DATA "─ARNHAM   ","|UILDFORD "," |EN
LEY      "
```

```
1310 REM
1320 REM SPRITE SHAPES SUBROUTINE
1330 FORSS=13TO192STEP179
1340 FORS=0TO62
1350 READ SP
1360 POKESS*64+S,SP
1370 NEXT:NEXT
1380 GOTO1690
1390 DATA 255,192,0
1400 DATA 255,192,0
1410 DATA 48,192,30
1420 DATA 48,192,30
1430 DATA 48,192,12
1440 DATA 48,192,12
1450 DATA 48,192,12
1460 DATA 48,195,12
1470 DATA 48,199,140
1480 DATA 48,194,140
1490 DATA 255,255,255
1500 DATA 255,255,255
1510 DATA 255,255,255
1520 DATA 255,255,255
1530 DATA 255,255,255
1540 DATA 255,255,255
1550 DATA 255,255,255
1560 DATA 255,255,255
1570 DATA 63,3,240
1580 DATA 63,3,240
1590 DATA 63,3,240
1600 REM
1610 DATA 0,0,24
1620 DATA 0,0,62
1630 DATA 0,0,127
1640 DATA 0,0,127
1650 DATA 0,0,63
1660 DATA 0,0,12
1670 DATA 0,0,0,0,0,0,0,0,0,0,0,0,0,0,0,
0,0,0,0,0,0,0,0,0,0,0,0,0,0,0,0,0,0
1680 DATA 0,0,0,0,0,0,0,0,0,0
1690 RETURN
1700 REM RIGHT SOUND SUBROUTINE
1710 POKEWV,33:POKEVL,15:POKEAD,190:POKE
SR,248
```

```
1720 POKES1,68:POKES2,149:FORTT=1TO200:N
EXTTT
1730 POKEWV,0:POKEVL,0:POKEAD,0
1740 RETURN
1750 REM CHUFFING NOISE SUBROUTINE
1760 POKEWV,129:POKEVL,15:POKEAD,15:POKE
SR,248
1770 POKES1,68:POKES2,149:FORTT=1TO20:NE
XTTT
1780 POKEWV,0:POKEVL,0:POKEAD,0
1790 RETURN
1800 REM END OF RUN SOUND SUBROUTINE
1810 POKEWV,33:POKEVL,15:POKEAD,190
1820 POKES1,25:POKES2,177:FORTT=1TO200:N
EXTTT
1830 POKES1,20:POKES2,100:FORTT=1TO200:N
EXTTT
1840 POKEWV,0:POKEVL,0:POKEAD,0
1850 RETURN
1860 END
```

WESTERN ADVENTURE GAME

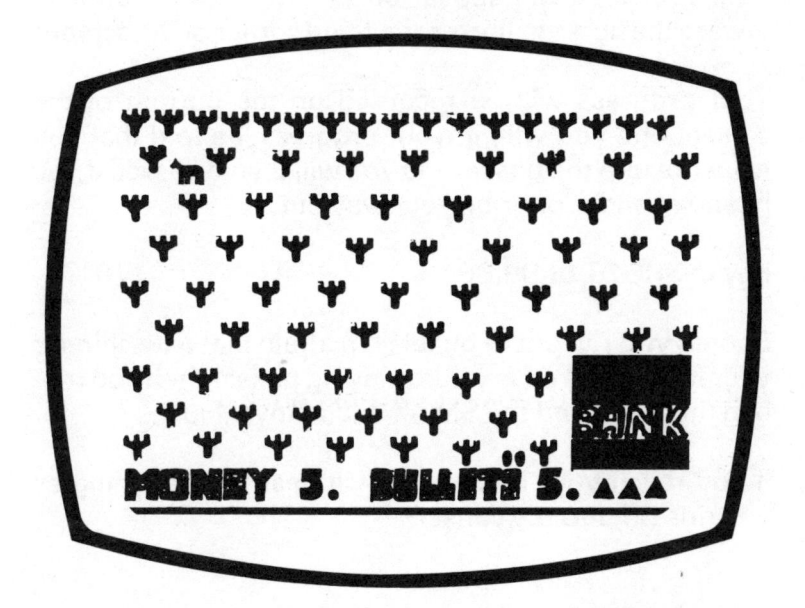

After robbing the bank, your rough, tough and ready desperado colleagues have fled into the scrubland, dropping their guns and the loot.

Well we all know that a man, or a Calamity Jane, has got to do what ever it is. So, you are on your own outside the bank and you have to make it to the horses, which some idiot left on the outskirts of town.

On the way you can collect money and guns with bullets and then decide, if you run into the Sheriff's posse, whether to bribe or blast your way to freedom. Obviously your aim is to reach the horses with some bullets and some money.

We are not advocating here that crime pays — that is up to you.

How to play

Use the ARROW keys to make your moves.

Your footsteps will appear on the screen as you move toward the horse in the top left hand corner of the screen.

Your progress will be recorded on the bottom of the screen, and you will, in your progress, be told that you have run into the posse, and you will then be asked if you intend to shoot or bribe your way out.

Key in SHOOT or BRIBE

Should you run out of bullets I'm afraid that a lynching is your fate, as the posse were playing poker when you robbed the bank, and the Sheriff had a Royal Flush.

If you reach your horse, you will hear the galloping as you ride off into the sunset.

Programming hints

This program shows how the attack and delay rate of the sound envelope changes the sound heard. For example gunshot has a fast attack and slow delay while the galloping sound has equal attack and delay rates.

You can increase the number of events in the adventure by allowing W on line 510 to be larger.

A procedure describing the event, and the effect of it, on the money and bullets can be written.

The new procedures can be listed after line 760.

Remember that

> BU is number of bullets
> MO is money
> X is the random amount to increase/decrease

Program

```
10 REM WESTERN ADVENTURE GAME
20 REM COPYRIGHT (C) G.LUDINSKI 1983
30 POKE53280,2:POKE53281,7:POKE53272,21:
REM BORDER BACKGROUND AND UPPER CASE
40 S1=54273:S2=54272:VL=54296:WV=54276:A
D=54277:REM SOUND VARIABLES
50 CM=55296:PM=1024:KL=40:REM COLOUR AND
 SCREEN MAP
60 HO$=CHR$(19):CL$=CHR$(147):CG$=CHR$(1
51):CD$=CHR$(17):CU$=CHR$(145)
70 CB$=CHR$(157):CF$=CHR$(29)
80 GR$=CHR$(30):RD$=CHR$(28):BL$=CHR$(14
4):R1$=CHR$(18):R0$=CHR$(146)
90 X0=28:Y0=16
100 PRINTCL$;CG$;
110 REM
120 REM CACTUS
130 REM
140 FORK=1TO3
150 PRINTGR$:FORI=1TO8:PRINTCHR$(167);CH
R$(167);CHR$(165);CHR$(165);" ";:NEXT
160 FORI=1TO8:PRINT" ";CHR$(112);CHR$(11
1);"  ";:NEXT
170 FORI=1TO8:PRINT" ";CHR$(167);CHR$(16
5);"  ";:NEXT
180 PRINT
190 NEXT
200 REM
210 REM DRAW BANK
220 REM
230 PRINTHO$:FORI=1TO14:PRINTCD$;:NEXT
240 PRINTRD$;
```

```
250 PRINTTAB(30);R1$;"         "
260 PRINTTAB(30);R1$;" BANK "
270 PRINTTAB(30);R1$;"          ";CG$
280 REM
290 REM HORSE
300 REM
310 PRINTHO$;BL$;TAB(2);"  ,"
320 PRINTHO$;CD$;TAB(2);CHR$(188);CHR$(1
91);CHR$(162);CHR$(105)
330 PRINTHO$;CD$;CD$;TAB(2);"   ";CHR$(1
67);CHR$(167);CG$
340 REM
350 REM WRITE MESSAGES
360 REM
370 BU=5:MO=5:DI=1
380 GOSUB770:PRINTSTR$(DI);")   MONEY =";
STR$(MO);", BULLETS =";STR$(BU)
390 IFX0=4ANDY0=0THENGOSUB900:GOTO1040
400 IFBU<=0THENPRINT"YOU GET SHOT.YOU HA
VE TRAVELLED ";DI;" YDS":GOSUB810:GOTO10
40
410 X=INT(RND(1)*5+2)
420 POKE198,0
430 GETTU$:IFTU$=""THENGOTO430
440 IFTU$<>CU$ANDTU$<>CD$ANDTU$<>CB$ANDT
U$<>CF$THENGOTO430
450 IFTU$=CB$THENX0=X0-1
460 IFTU$=CF$THENX0=X0+1
470 IFTU$=CD$THENY0=Y0+1
480 IFTU$=CU$THENY0=Y0-1
490 POKECM+(KL*Y0)+X0,12:POKEPM+(KL*Y0)+
X0,81
500 DI=DI+1
510 W=INT(RND(1)*4+1)
520 IFW=1THENGOSUB570
530 IFW=2THENGOSUB670
540 IFW=3THENGOSUB720
550 GOTO380
560 REM
570 REM POSSE SUBROUTINE
580 PRINT"YOU MEET ONE OF THE SHERIFF'S
POSSE. DO YOU SHOOT OR BRIBE "
```

```
590 INPUTI$
600 IFI$<>"SHOOT"ANDI$<>"SHOOT"ANDI$<>"B
RIBE"ANDI$<>"BRIBE"THENPRINTCU$;CU$:GOTO
590
610 IFI$="SHOOT"THENGOSUB810:BU=BU-X
620 IFI$="BRIBE"THENMO=MO-X
630 IFBU<0THENBU=0
640 IFMO<0THENMO=0
650 PRINTCU$;
660 RETURN
670 REM BULLETS SUBROUTINE
680 PRINT"YOU FIND";X;" BULLETS THAT YOU
R GANG LEFT BEHIND"
690 BU=BU+X
700 FORK=1TO800:NEXTK
710 RETURN
720 REM MONEY SUBROUTINE
730 PRINT"YOU FIND";X;" BAGS OF MONEY TH
AT YOUR GANGLEFT BEHIND"
740 MO=MO+X
750 FORK=1TO800:NEXTK
760 RETURN
770 REM BLANK SUBROUTINE
780 PRINTHO$:FORK=1TO18:PRINTCD$;:NEXT:F
ORI=1TO190:PRINT" ";:NEXTI
790 PRINTCU$;CU$;CU$;CU$;CU$;CU$
800 RETURN
810 REM GUN SHOT SUBROUTINE
820 POKEWV,129:POKEAD,15
830 FORVO=15TO0STEP-1
840 POKEVL,VO
850 POKES1,40:POKES2,200
860 FORTT=1TO10:NEXTTT
870 NEXT
880 POKEWV,0:POKEAD,0
890 RETURN
900 REM GALLOPING SOUND SUBROUTINE
910 POKEWV,129:POKEAD,170:POKES1,68:POKE
S2,149
920 FORJ=1TO10
930 POKEVL,15:FORTT=1TO80:NEXTTT
940 POKEVL,0:FORTT=1TO10:NEXTTT
```

```
950 FORK=1TO2
960 POKEVL,10:FORTT=1TO50:NEXTTT
970 POKEVL,0:FORTT=1TO50:NEXTTT
980 NEXTK
990 POKEVL,15:FORTT=1TO60:NEXTTT
1000 POKEVL,0:FORTT=1TO200:NEXTTT
1010 POKEWV,0:POKEAD,0
1020 NEXT
1030 RETURN
1040 END
```

DETECTIVE

Could you solve the cases and survive the perils of being a detective. Find out by playing this game.

Firstly, you are briefed on the correct number-plates for the cars and trucks you are likely to see. Then you are stationed near a main road, watching cars and vans travel past.

You are looking for a stolen vehicle whose plates have been changed. When you see a car or van you suspect, you must call up, by radio, the two squad cars in the area, and tell them to set up a road-block.

If you time it right, the suspected vehicle, which veers off the road when it sees you are interested, will be caught. If your suspected vehicle was stolen and you catch it, the driver comes quietly and your score increases. If however, you catch a vehicle which has not been stolen, the driver dresses you down, and your score decreases. If you do not catch the suspected vehicle, then you are told whether your suspicions were correct but your score is unchanged.

How to play

Press C when you have read which cars and vans have which number plates. Then you see cars and vans travel by with the number plates they have attached to them displayed below the road. When you see a vehicle which you suspect has the wrong number plate, then press A to get the black car at the top of the screen to set up a road block, or Z to have the black car below it set up a trap. You may do this continuously, by trying to set up the road block just as the suspected vehicle passes by.

If you catch the vehicle you will hear police-car sirens as the other squad cars approach. Then you are told the result. Press the RETURN key to play again.

If while watching the cars travel past, you forget what the correct number plates are, then press D to return to the Duty Roster.

Programming hints

The cars and vans are made up of two sprites. They are animated, or made to travel along the road, in lines 380 to 440. They are animated by increasing the value of X, and drawing the sprite in the new position.

You can make the game more difficult by making the vehicles whizz past faster. To do this increase the STEP size in line 380.

Program

```
10 REM DETECTIVE
20 REM COPYRIGHT (C) G.LUDINSKI 1983
30 POKE53280,2:POKE53281,12:POKE53272,21
:REM BORDER BACKGROUND AND UPPER CASE
40 DIMV$(6),C(6),P(6),VM$(6)
50 HO$=CHR$(19):CL$=CHR$(147):CG$=CHR$(1
51):CU$=CHR$(145):CD$=CHR$(17)
60 BL$=CHR$(144):YE$=CHR$(158):WH$=CHR$(
5):RD$=CHR$(28):BU$=CHR$(31)
70 R1$=CHR$(18):R0$=CHR$(146)
80 S1=54273:S2=54272:VL=54296:WV=54276:A
D=54277:REM SOUND VARIABLES
90 M1$="IT'S A FAIR COP,GUV."
100 RO$="":FORK=1TO20:RO$=RO$+CHR$(185):
NEXT
110 V=53248:POKEV+21,31:REM ENABLE SPRIT
ES
120 POKE2040,13:POKE2041,192:FORK=2TO4:P
OKE2040+K,13:NEXT:REM SPRITE DATA AREA
130 GOSUB1100
140 DEF FNR(MAX)=INT(RND(1)*MAX+1)
150 C(1)=1:P(1)=0:C(2)=2:P(2)=0:C(3)=6:P
(3)=0:SC=0
160 FORI=1TO3:C(I+3)=C(I):P(I+3)=1:NEXT
170 GOSUB610
180 REM
190 REM DRAW FIELDS,ROAD,POLICE CARS
200 REM
210 POKE53281,5:PRINTCL$;WH$;
220 FORK=1TO10:PRINTCD$;:NEXT
230 FORK=1TO5:PRINTCHR$(152);R1$;"
                                     ";:NEXT
240 PRINTR0$
250 GOSUB790
260 MX=0
270 CL=0:S=2:X=30:Y=60:GOSUB1480
280 CL=0:S=3:X=30:Y=85:GOSUB1480
290 CL=0:S=4:X=30:Y=200:GOSUB1480
300 PRINTHO$;:FORK=1TO18:PRINTCD$;:NEXT
```

```
310 PRINTWH$;"CALL UP SQUAD CARS A OR Z
FOR ROAD-BLOCK"
320 PRINT:PRINTTAB(20);"SCORE ";STR$(SC)
330 REM
340 REM LET CARS TRAVEL ALONG ROAD
350 REM
360 MX=0
370 J=FNR(6)
380 FORI=30TO320STEP5
390 PRINTHO$;:FORII=1TO16:PRINTCD$;:NEXT
:PRINTWH$;R1$;TAB(16);VM$(J)
400 CL=C(J):S=P(J):Y=138
410 GETI$:IFI$=""THENX=I:GOSUB1480:GOTO4
40
420 IFI$="D"THENGOSUB610:GOTO210
430 GOTO470
440 NEXT
450 Y=250:GOSUB1480
460 GOTO370
470 GOSUB860
480 REM
490 REM FINAL MESSAGE AND POLICE SIREN
500 REM
510 GOSUB1540
520 PRINTCG$;
530 PRINTHO$;:FORJJ=1TO21:PRINTCD$;:NEXT
540 IFEN=1AND(VN$=VM$(A)ORVN$=VM$(BB))TH
ENSC=SC+1:PRINT:PRINTM1$:GOTO580
550 IFEN=1THENPRINT:PRINT"I'LL SUE YOU,Y
OU B**":SC=SC-1:GOTO580
560 IFVN$=VM$(A)ORVN$=VM$(BB)THENPRINT:P
RINT"THE STOLEN CAR HAS GONE ":GOTO580
570 PRINT:PRINT"YOU HAVE BEEN CHASING TH
E WRONG CAR "
580 POKE198,0
590 PRINT"PRESS RETURN            ";:INPUTRB
$:GOTO170
600 REM
610 REM START SUBROUTINE
620 FORS=0TO4:Y=29:GOSUB1480:NEXT
630 PRINTCL$;CG$;
640 FORI=1TO6
```

```
650 V$(I)=CHR$(64+FNR(26))+CHR$(64+FNR(2
6))+CHR$(64+FNR(26))
660 FORK=1TO3:V$(I)=V$(I)+RIGHT$(STR$(FN
R(10)-1),1):NEXT
670 V$(I)=V$(I)+CHR$(64+FNR(26))
680 NEXT
690 PRINT:PRINTTAB(6);"DUTY ROSTER FOR P
.C. HOLMES":PRINT:PRINT
700 PRINT:PRINTTAB(11);CG$;"WHITE CAR ";
V$(1)
710 PRINT:PRINTTAB(11);RD$;"RED CAR    ";
V$(2)
720 PRINT:PRINTTAB(11);BU$;"BLUE CAR   ";
V$(3)
730 PRINT:PRINTTAB(11);CG$;"WHITE VAN ";
V$(4)
740 PRINT:PRINTTAB(11);RD$;"RED VAN    ";
V$(5)
750 PRINT:PRINTTAB(11);BU$;"BLUE VAN   ";
V$(6)
760 PRINT:PRINT:PRINTCG$;"PRESS C TO CON
TINUE"
770 GETRB$:IFRB$=""THENGOTO770
780 RETURN
790 REM MIX SUBROUTINE
800 A=FNR(6):BB=FNR(6):IFBB=A THENGOTO80
0
810 FORI=1TO6
820 VM$(I)=V$(I)
830 NEXTI
840 WK$=VM$(A):VM$(A)=VM$(BB):VM$(BB)=WK
$
850 RETURN
860 REM CHASE SUBROUTINE
870 CL=C(J):VT=P(J):VN$=VM$(J)
880 X=24:MX=0:Y=130:GS=0:EN=0
890 GETI$
900 IFI$="A"THENRD=2:GOSUB1030
910 IFI$="Z"THENRD=5:GOSUB1030
920 IFEN=1THENGOTO1020
930 S=VT:GOSUB1480
940 GETI$
```

```
950 IFI$="A"THENRD=2:GOSUB1030
960 IFI$="Z"THENRD=5:GOSUB1030
970 X=X+10:IFX>=255THENX=X-255:MX=MX+2↑V
T
980 IFMX>0ANDX>85THENMX=0:X=24
990 Y=Y-((-1)↑FNR(2))*INT(20*RND(1))-5:I
FY<30THENY=130
1000 IFY>130THENY=130
1010 GS=GS+1:IFGS<50THENGOTO890
1020 RETURN
1030 REM ROAD-BLOCK SUBROUTINE
1040 PRINTHO$;:FORJJ=1TORD:PRINTCD$;:NEX
T
1050 PRINTRD$;TAB(5);RO$
1060 PRINTCU$;TAB(5);"
  "
1070 IFRD=2AND(Y>55ANDY<65)THENEN=1
1080 IFRD=5AND(Y>80ANDY<90)THENEN=1
1090 RETURN
1100 REM SPRITE SHAPES SUBROUTINE
1110 RESTORE
1120 FORSS=13TO192STEP179
1130 FORS=0TO62
1140 READ SP
1150 POKESS*64+S,SP
1160 NEXT:NEXT
1170 GOTO1470
1180 DATA 0,0,0,0,0,0,0,0,0,0,0,0,0,0,0,
0,0,0,0,0,0,0,0,0
1190 DATA 0,127,128
1200 DATA 0,255,192
1210 DATA 1,128,96
1220 DATA 3,0,48
1230 DATA 63,255,255
1240 DATA 63,255,255
1250 DATA 63,255,255
1260 DATA 63,255,255
1270 DATA 3,192,30
1280 DATA 1,128,12
1290 DATA 0,0,0,0,0,0,0,0,0
1300 REM
1310 DATA 0,0,0,0,0,0,0,0,0,0,0,0
```

```
1320 DATA 255,252,0
1330 DATA 255,252,0
1340 DATA 255,252,0
1350 DATA 255,252,0
1360 DATA 255,255,128
1370 DATA 255,255,192
1380 DATA 255,252,96
1390 DATA 255,252,48
1400 DATA 255,255,255
1410 DATA 255,255,255
1420 DATA 255,255,255
1430 DATA 255,255,255
1440 DATA 3,192,30
1450 DATA 1,128,12
1460 DATA 0,0,0,0,0,0,0,0,0
1470 RETURN
1480 REM SPRITE POSITION SUBROUTINE
1490 POKEV+39+S,CL
1500 MX=0:IFX>255THENMX=MX+2↑S:X=X-255
1510 POKEV+2*S,X:POKEV+16,MX
1520 POKEV+2*S+1,Y
1530 RETURN
1540 REM POLICE SIREN SOUND SUBROUTINE
1550 POKEWV,17:POKEVL,15:POKEAD,190
1560 FORK=1TO4
1570 POKES1,38:POKES2,126:FORT=1TO300:NE
XT
1580 POKES1,34:POKES2,75:FORT=1TO300:NEX
T
1590 NEXTK
1600 POKEWV,0:POKEAD,0
1610 RETURN
```

BAR CHARTER

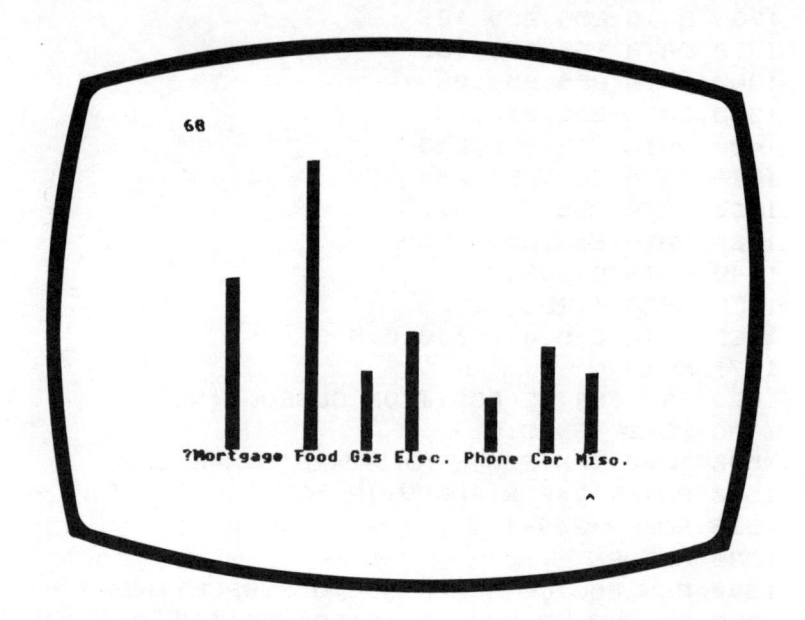

This is a versatile program that will enable you to record your expenses, club accounts or any collections you have. You could also use the printouts to impress the boss. It is easy to use and allows a maximum of 40 bars to be drawn of any height and in different colours. As you key in data you watch the bar chart grow. After you have done this, you have an option of printing out the bar chart on your printer. After this the height of each is displayed.

How to use it

First you are asked for the labels of the bars in the bar chart. There may be any number but all the labels must fit on one display line. When you have keyed in a line of labels press RETURN once. Then you use the left and right ARROW keys to move a pointer at the bottom of the screen. When the pointer (symbol ↑) is positioned under the label you wish to point to, press the space bar and the bar above that label will increase in height. Each time you press the space bar, the number at the top left hand side of the screen increases by one.

If a bar gets so high that it would go off the screen, then the entire bar chart moves downwards so you are looking at the top half of the bar chart. The keyboard is disabled while this happens.

If you want to print out the bar chart onto a printer, if you have one, press P, put the appropriate screen dump routine after line 550. Your dealer, computer magazine or the maker should be able to help you.

If you want to miss out the print out and go straight to the next stage, press S. This section prints out the total for each item of the bar chart.

Programming hints

The program incorporates a scroll downwards. If you list a program, you will notice that if the program has more than around 21 lines the screen scrolls upwards. The screen can be made to scroll downwards by filling each screen line with the contents of the line above it. Everything on the screen will now move down one screen line.

The bars in every four columns are different from those in the previous four columns. This is done by marking the colour poked to the screen in the poke-to-screen subroutine equal to a quarter of the column number X/4.

The colours can be changed to one or different colours by changing the INT (X/4) in this subroutine. The best colours to choose from are:

0	Black	6	Blue
1	White	7	Yellow
2	Red	8	Orange
3	Cyan	9	Brown
4	Purple	10	Pink
5	Green	11	Grey

Program

```
10 REM BAR CHARTER
20 REM COPYRIGHT (C) G.LUDINSKI 1983
30 POKE53280,2:POKE53281,12:REM BORDER A
ND BACKGROUND
32 S$="                                        "
40 DIMY(40)
50 POKE53272,21:REM UPPER CASE
60 HO$=CHR$(19):CL$=CHR$(147):CG$=CHR$(1
51):CU$=CHR$(145)
62 CM=55296:PM=1024:CL=40:REM COLOUR AND
 SCREEN MAP
70 PRINTCL$;CG$;
80 LA$=CHR$(157):RA$=CHR$(29)
90 REM
100 REM INPUT LABELS
110 REM
120 XT=10:YT=22:P$="WHAT ARE THE LABELS"
:GOSUB710
122 PRINTHO$:FORI=1TO22:PRINT:NEXT
130 INPUTL$:IFL$=""THENPRINTCU$;:GOTO130
140 IFLEN(L$)>40THENP$=S$:XT=0:YT=23:GOS
UB710
150 XT=0:YT=22:P$=S$:GOSUB710
160 S=0:X=1:X1=1:FORI=1TO40:Y(I)=22:NEXT
 I
170 PRINTHO$:PRINT" 0":POKE56257,11:POKE
1985,30
```

```
180 SC=0:DT=0
190 REM
200 REM KEY IN DATA
210 REM
212 S=0
220 S=S+1
230 GETI$:IFI$=""THENGOTO230
232 IFI$<>LA$ANDI$<>RA$ANDI$<>"S"ANDI$<>
" "ANDI$<>"P"THENGOTO230
240 IF(I$=LA$ANDX=1)OR(I$=RA$ANDX=40)THE
NGOTO230
250 IFI$=" "THENDT=DT+1:PRINTHO$:PRINTDT
260 IFI$=LA$THENX1=X:X=X-1
270 IFI$=RA$THENX1=X:X=X+1
280 POKE56256+X,11:POKE1984+X1,32:POKE19
84+X,30
290 REM
300 REM SCROLL DOWN IF CHART GOES TOO HI
GH
310 REM
320 IFY(X)+SC>=0THENGOTO370
322 GOSUB790
330 PRINTHO$;S$:PRINTDT:P$=L$:XT=0:YT=23
:GOSUB710:SC=SC+1
340 REM
350 REM ADD MORE TO BAR
360 REM
370 IFI$<>" "THENGOTO410
390 YT=Y(X)+SC:IFYT>22THENYT=22
400 XT=X:P$=CHR$(224):GOSUB710:Y(X)=Y(X)
-1
410 IFI$<>"S"ANDI$<>"P"THENGOTO220
420 IFI$="P"THENGOSUB550
430 REM
440 REM TOTALS
450 REM
460 PRINTCL$;
470 PRINTHO$:PRINTTAB(17);"TOTALS":PRINT
TAB(17);"————":PRINT
480 FORI=1TO40
490 PRINTMID$(L$,I,1);" ";:IF22-Y(I)<>0T
HENPRINT22-Y(I);
```

```
500 PRINT
510 IFI=22THENPRINT:PRINT"PRESS RETURN TO CONTINUE";:INPUTRB$:PRINTCL$:PRINT
520 NEXTI
540 GOTO700
550 REM SCREEN DUMP SUBROTINE
690 RETURN
700 END
710 REM POKE TO SCREEN SUBROUTINE
720 FORF=XTTOXT+LEN(P$)-1
730 SD=(CL*YT)+F
732 IFP$=CHR$(224)THENPOKECM+SD,INT(F/4):GOTO750
740 POKECM+SD,11
750 CC$=MID$(P$,F-XT+1,1):IFCC$=" "THENPOKEPM+SD,32:GOTO770
760 POKEPM+SD,ASC(CC$)-64
770 NEXTF
780 RETURN
790 REM SCROLL DOWN SUBROUTINE
800 FORJ=1943TO1064STEP-1
810 POKEJ,PEEK(J-40)
820 NEXT
830 RETURN
```

STATS PAINTER

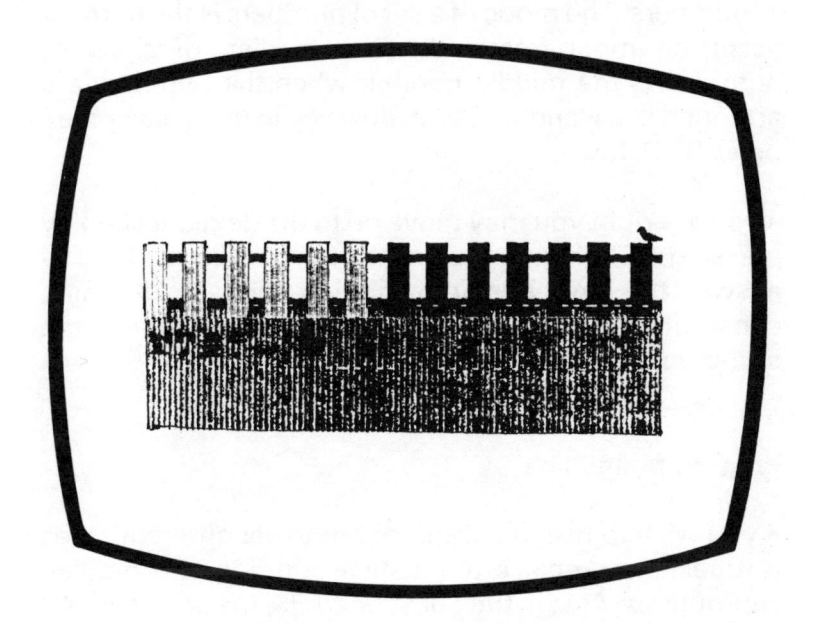

You are the director of Rockets Unlimited, and yesterday you were very pleased in the way the company was going. Then these officious accountants came, studied the figures and reckoned you were making a loss.

All weekend the sales figures are preying on your mind. Even while you are painting the fence you are trying to find out where the accountants went wrong. Sometimes you get so lost in thought that you end up painting the bird on the fence. If you do, it chirps in disapproval. If you can work accurately and quickly, you will find out where the accountants went wrong, and you will be able to prove to them that Rockets Unlimited is the success you always knew it was.

How to play

The questions are on the modes or medians of a given set of numbers. The mode of a set of numbers is the number occurring most frequently. The median of a set of numbers is the middle number when the numbers are arranged in ascending order. Just key in the answer then press RETURN.

If you are right you may move on to the next question by pressing RETURN. If you are wrong, or take too long to answer, the bird ends up by getting painted. After nine consecutive correct answers you find out where the accountants went wrong.

Programming hints

If you wish to use the graphics but to set different types of questions, replace the statistics, mode and median subroutines. Assign the question to Q$, the answer to A$ and the hint to H$. Questions in this program must have answers one digit or letter long. This could be changed, though, by changing the input routine at line 460.

Program

```
10 REM STATS PAINTER
20 REM COPYRIGHT (C) G.LUDINSKI 1983
30 POKE53280,5:POKE53281,6:POKE53272,21:
REM BORDER,BACKGROUND AND UPPER CASE
40 DIMD(15),C(5)
50 HO$=CHR$(19):CL$=CHR$(147):CG$=CHR$(1
51):RD$=CHR$(28):WH$=CHR$(5)
60 CD$=CHR$(17):CU$=CHR$(145)
70 S$="        "
80 PRINTCL$;WH$;
```

```
90 PRINTHO$;:FORI=1TO12:PRINTCD$;:NEXT:P
RINT"        PLEASE WAIT WHILE I THINK "
100 CM=55296:PM=1024:KL=40:REM COLOUR AN
D SCREEN MAP
110 GOTO230
120 REM
130 REM U.D.G. CALCULATOR SUBROUTINE
140 REM
150 TF=0
160 FORL=0TO7
170 TF=TF+(2↑L)*VAL(MID$(N$,8-L,1))
180 NEXTL
190 RETURN
200 REM
210 REM BIRD SHAPE
220 REM
230 Z$="01100000110000000110000001110000
"
240 Z$=Z$+"0011110000011110000010110000 1
011"
250 FORI=0TO7
260 N$=MID$(Z$,I*8+1,8)
270 GOSUB130:A(I)=TF
280 NEXTI
290 GOSUB1050
300 REM
310 REM DRAW FENCE
320 REM
330 FORJ=1TO9
340 PRINTCL$;
350 CO=5:X=0:Y=24:W=40:H=10:GOSUB580
360 FORK=0TO36STEP3
370 CO=1:X=K:Y=14:W=2:H=6:GOSUB580
380 NEXTK
390 CO=1:X=2:Y=10:W=36:H=1:GOSUB580:Y=13
:GOSUB580
400 PRINTHO$;:FORH=1TO8:PRINTCD$;:NEXT
410 PRINTLEFT$(S$,36);CHR$(35)
420 GOSUB670
430 PRINTHO$;:FORI=1TO16:PRINTCD$;:NEXT
440 PRINTQ$
```

```
450 I=-3:I$="":ID=0
460 GETI$:IFI$=""ORID=1THENI=I+3:CO=2:X=
I:Y=14:W=2:H=6:GOSUB580
470 IFI<34AND(I$=""ORID=1)THENGOTO460
480 IFI$=A$ANDID=0THENPRINT:PRINT:PRINT"
YES,YOU ARE RIGHT":GOTO520
490 IFI<34THENPRINTI$;:ID=1:GOTO460
500 GOSUB960
510 PRINT:PRINT"NO,";H$
520 PRINT:PRINT"HIT RETURN FOR MORE";:IN
PUTRB$
530 IFI$<>A$THENGOTO340
540 NEXTJ
550 PRINTHO$;:FORI=1TO15:PRINTCD$;:NEXT
560 PRINT"EUREKA! YOU FOUND IT.GET ON TH
E PHONE    QUICK":GOTO1040
570 REM
580 REM BLOCK SUBROUTINE
590 FORX1=XTOX+W-1
600 FORY1=Y-H+1TOY
610 SD=(Y1*KL)+X1
620 POKECM+SD,CO
630 POKEPM+SD,38
640 NEXT
650 NEXT
660 RETURN
670 REM STATISTICS SUBROUTINE
680 MC=0:DN=1:MO=0:W=INT(RND(1)*2+1)
690 FORI=1TO5
700 C(I)=INT(RND(1)*4):IFC(I)=MCTHENGOTO
700
710 IFC(I)>MCTHENMC=C(I):MO=I
720 IFC(I)=0THENGOTO770
730 FORJJ=DNTODN+C(I)-1
740 D(JJ)=I
750 NEXTJJ
760 DN=DN+C(I)
770 NEXTI
780 IFDN/2=INT(DN/2)THENDN=DN+1:D(DN)=6
790 D$="":FORI=1TODN:D$=D$+STR$(D(I)):NE
XT
```

```
800 TH$="TH":MM=INT(DN/2)+1:IFMM=1THENTH
$="ST"
810 IFMM=2THENTH$="ND"
820 IFMM=3THENTH$="RD"
830 IFW=1THENGOSUB860
840 IFW=2THENGOSUB910
850 RETURN
860 REM MODE SUBROUTINE
870 Q$="WHAT IS THE MODE OF"+D$
880 A=MO:A$=STR$(MO):A$=RIGHT$(A$,LEN(A$
)-1)
890 H$="THERE ARE MORE "+A$+"S"
900 RETURN
910 REM MEDIAN SUBROUTINE
920 Q$="WHAT IS THE MEDIAN OF"+D$
930 A=D(1+INT(DN/2)):A$=STR$(A):A$=RIGHT
$(A$,LEN(A$)-1)
940 H$=A$+" IS MIDDLE NO."
950 RETURN
960 REM BIRD SONG SUBROUTINE
970 POKE54296,15:POKE54277,15:POKE54276,
17:POKE54278,244
980 FORJK=1TO6
990 POKE54296,15:POKE54273,244:POKE54272
,103:FORK=1TO100:NEXTK
1000 POKE54296,0:FORK=1TO020:NEXT
1010 NEXTJK
1020 POKE54276,0:POKE54277,0:POKE54278,0
1030 RETURN
1040 END
1050 REM DEFINE BIRD SHAPE SUBROUTINE
1060 POKE56334,PEEK(56334)AND254:POKE1,P
EEK(1)AND251
1070 FORI=0TO63
1080 FORJ=0TO7
1090 POKE12288+I*8+J,PEEK(53248+I*8+J)
1100 NEXTJ
1110 NEXTI
1120 POKE1,PEEK(1)OR4:POKE56334,PEEK(563
34)OR1
1130 POKE53272,(PEEK(53272)AND240)+12
```

```
1140 REM
1150 REM REDEFINE HASH TO BIRD SHAPE
1160 REM
1170 CG=12568
1180 FORI=0TO7
1190 POKECG+I,A(I)
1200 NEXT
1210 REM
1220 REM REDEFINE AMPERSAND TO BLOCK
1230 REM
1240 CG=12592
1250 FORI=0TO7:POKECG+I,255:NEXT
1260 RETURN
```

WHO DUNNIT

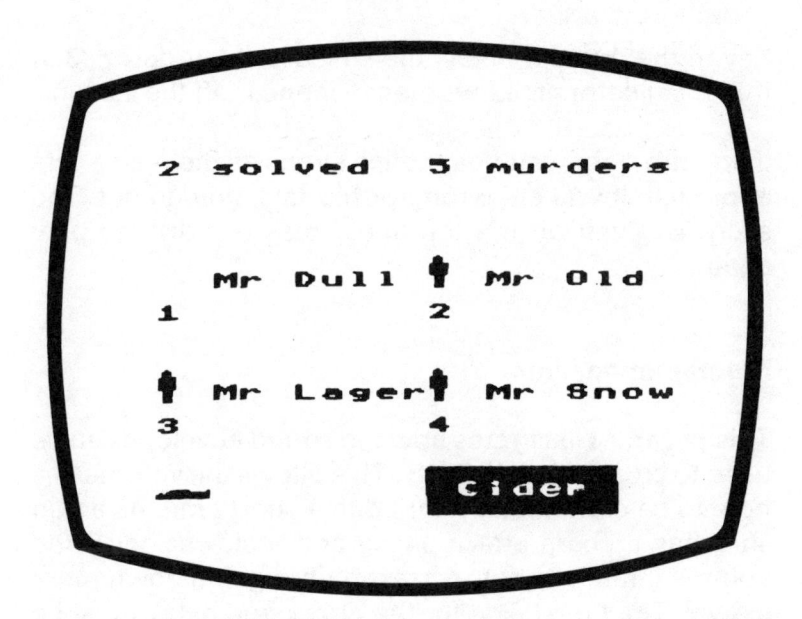

```
2 solved   5 murders

      Mr Dull  ♦  Mr Old
   1            2

   ♦  Mr Lager ♦ Mr Snow
   3            4

                  Cider
```

Looking through the window you see him standing in his study. Then you hear a gun shot and he falls to the ground. You walk into the house and go into his study.

There are four men there. You know their names. You find a note which he must have written before he died. This is a clue to the murderer. You must decide which of the four men is the murderer before they slip out the room.

How to play

The victim's note is by the man lying down. You must work out which of the names of the other men has some connection with this word. For example, in the screen show above, Mr Lager is the murderer as Lager and Cider are both drinks. Alternatively words that are related may have the same or opposite meanings. For example, Big and Large, also Hot and Cold are related.

Key in the number below the suspected murderer, (3 in this case) before the four men disappear off the screen.

If you are right, you hear police sirens as the police cars approach. If you are wrong or too late, you do not. The score is given on the top line. Press RETURN to play again.

Programming hints

This program illustrates how the sound envelope can be used to create sound effects. This allows the volume of a note to be continuously varied in a short time. As a gun shot has a sharp attack phase and a slower delay the volume initially shoots up fast before going down more slowly. The time taken for the attack and delay must be given a value between 0 and 15, with 0 representing a fast attack/delay and 15 a slow one. Then multiply the attack value by 16 and add the delay value. Then POKE this value into AD. So for gun shot we POKE (0 x 16) + 15 into AD, i.e. 15.

If you want to add more words to the game, add some more DATA statements at the end of the program. Put in sets of three words that are related. Read the other words in lines 840 to 890 for ideas. Make sure that each set is not related to the other words in those lines. When you have added the extra words, count up the total number of sets of words from line 840 and assign it to TT in line 230.

Program

```
10 REM WHODUNNIT
20 REM COPYRIGHT (C) G.LUDINSKI 1983
30 POKE53280,2:POKE53281,12:POKE53272,21
```

```
:REM BORDER BACKGROUND AND UPPER CASE
40 S1=54273:S2=54272:VL=54296:WV=54276:A
D=54277:REM SOUND VARIABLES
50 CM=55296:PM=1024:KL=40:REM COLOUR AND
 SCREEN MAP
60 HO$=CHR$(19):CL$=CHR$(147):CG$=CHR$(1
51):CD$=CHR$(17):CU$=CHR$(145)
70 CB$=CHR$(157):R1$=CHR$(18):R0$=CHR$(1
46)
80 RD$=CHR$(28):YE$=CHR$(158):WH$=CHR$(5
):BL$=CHR$(144)
90 DIMWD$(30,3),N(5),X(4),Y(4),P1$(2),P2
$(2)
100 DEF FNRN(MAX)=INT(RND(1)*MAX+1)
110 S$="
          "
120 X(1)=2:Y(1)=7:X(2)=20:Y(2)=7:X(3)=2:
Y(3)=14:X(4)=20:Y(4)=14
130 SC=0:TU=0
140 REM
150 REM SHAPES OF MEN
160 REM
170 M$=CHR$(119)+CD$+CB$+CB$+R1$+CHR$(16
1)+R0$+" "+CHR$(161)+CD$+CB$+CB$+R1$+" "
180 M$=M$+R0$
190 V$=CHR$(119)+CHR$(162)+CHR$(162)+CHR
$(185)+CHR$(187)
200 REM
210 REM READ WORDS
220 REM
230 TT=25
240 FORII=1TOTT
250 READWD$(II,1),WD$(II,2),WD$(II,3)
260 NEXTII
270 TI$="000000"
280 REM
290 REM UPRIGHT MAN AND GUN SHOT
300 REM
310 PRINTCL$;BL$;
320 FORI=1TO4
330 N(I)=FNRN(TT)
340 NEXTI
350 IFN(1)=N(2)ORN(1)=N(3)ORN(1)=N(4)ORN
(2)=N(3)ORN(2)=N(4)THENGOTO320
```

```
360 IFN(3)=N(4)THENGOTO320
370 FORK=1TO20:PRINTCD$;:NEXT:PRINTTAB(2
);M$
380 GOSUB900
390 REM
400 REM DRAW PEOPLE AND NAMES
410 REM
420 TU=TU+1
430 SN=FNRN(4)
440 FORI=1TO2
450 P1$(I)=WD$(N((2*I)-1),FNRN(3)):P2$(I
)=WD$(N(2*I),FNRN(3))
460 PRINTHO$;:FORK=1TO7*I:PRINTCD$;:NEXT
:PRINTBL$;TAB(2);M$;RD$;"  MR. ";P1$(I);
470 PRINTCU$;CU$;
480 PRINTBL$;TAB(20);M$;RD$;"  MR. ";P2$
(I)
490 PRINTCD$;TAB(2);2*I-1;TAB(20);2*I
500 NEXTI
510 VC$=WD$(N(SN),FNRN(3))
520 IFVC$=P1$(1)ORVC$=P2$(1)ORVC$=P1$(2)
ORVC$=P2$(2)THENGOTO510
530 MU$=" "+VC$+" "
540 PRINTHO$;:FORK=1TO20:PRINTCD$;:NEXT:
PRINT"               "
550 PRINTCU$;BL$;TAB(2);V$;RD$;R1$;TAB(2
0);LEFT$(S$,LEN(MU$))
560 PRINTTAB(1);"    ";TAB(20);R1$;MU$:PR
INTTAB(2);" ";TAB(20);R1$;
570 PRINTLEFT$(S$,LEN(MU$))
580 K=1
590 GETI$:IFI$<>""ORK>4THENGOTO670
600 FORJ=0TO2:POKECM+(KL*(Y(K)+J))+X(K),
12:NEXTJ
610 POKECM+(KL*(Y(K)+1))+X(K)-1,12:POKEC
M+(KL*(Y(K)+1))+X(K)+1,12
620 K=K+1
630 FORT=1TO300:NEXTT:GOTO590
640 REM
650 REM POLICE SIREN
660 REM
670 IFVAL(I$)<>SNTHENGOTO770
```

```
680 POKEVL,15:POKEAD,190:POKEWV,17
690 FORK=1TO4
700 POKES1,38:POKES2,126:FORT=1TO300:NEX
T
710 POKES1,34:POKES2,75:FORT=1TO300:NEXT
720 NEXTK
730 POKEWV,0:POKEAD,0:SC=SC+1
740 REM
750 REM SCORE
760 REM
770 PRINTHO$;CG$;TAB(10);STR$(SC);" SOLV
ED";TAB(10);STR$(TU);
780 IFTU>1THENPRINT" MURDERS"
790 IFTU=1THENPRINT" MURDER"
800 PRINTHO$;:FORL=1TO23:PRINTCD$;:NEXT:
POKE198,0:PRINT"PRESS RETURN";
810 INPUTRB$:GOTO310
820 REM DATA
830 REM
840 DATA BIG,SMALL,LARGE,FAT,THIN,PLUMP,
QUIET,LOUD,NOISY,WET,DRY,DAMP
850 DATA HOT,COLD,WARM,A,Z,ALPHA,GOOD,BA
D,NICE,MAD,CRAZY,SANE,DULL,SHINY,MATT
860 DATA SEE,HEAR,FEEL,OLD,YOUNG,AGED,LA
UGH,CRY,WEEP,KID,CHILD,ADULT,AM,PM,NOON
870 DATA BIRD,FOWL,BEAST,SNOW,ICE,SLEET,
BEER,LAGER,CIDER
880 DATA KING,QUEEN,JACK,GIVE,TAKE,GRASP
,BBC,ITV,CH. 4,ILL,WELL,SICK,GYM,PT,PE
890 DATA RED,AMBER,GREEN,LOAD,SAVE,RUN,E
YE,I,AYE
900 REM GUN SHOT SUBROUTINE
910 POKEWV,129:POKEAD,15
920 FORVO=15TO0STEP-1
930 POKEVL,VO
940 POKES1,40:POKES2,200
950 FORTT=1TO10:NEXTTT
960 NEXTVO
970 POKEWV,0:POKEAD,0
980 RETURN
```

WORD SEARCH

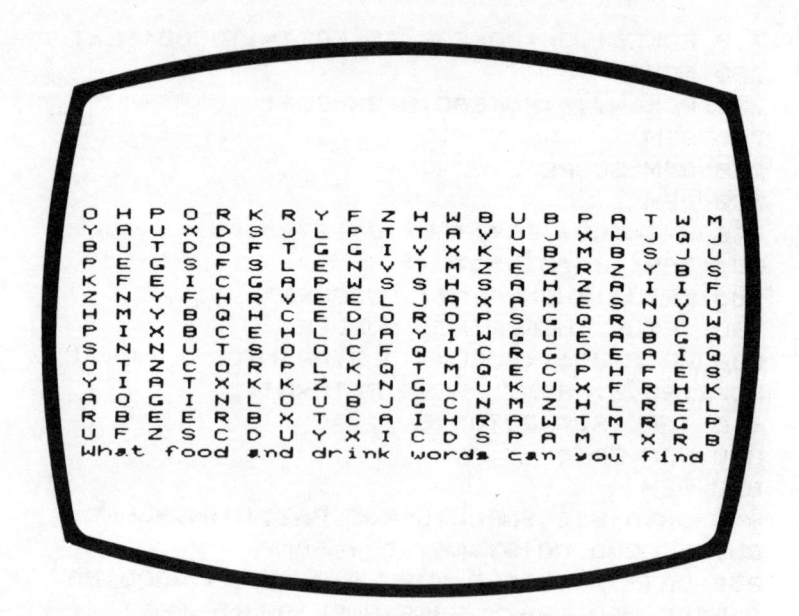

```
O H P O R K R Y F Z H W B U B P A T W M
Y A U X D S J L P T A V U J X H R J J U
B U T D O F T G G I V X K N B M B S Q S
P E G S F L E N V T Y E Z R Z Y I B I T
K F E I C G A P W S S M H A A T N V F U
Z N Y F H R V E E L J H X A H M E U W W
H M Y B Q C E E H O P S G Q E R N J A A
P I X B C E L U A Y I W G U A A O G Q Q
S N I O T O C F Q T M Q R E D P B I S
O T Z Z O R P L K O M Q E C P H F E R
Y I A T X K K Z J N G G U U X F R H L
A O G I N L O U B J C N M Z H L R E P
R B E E R B X T C A I H R A W T M R G R
U F Z S C D U Y X I C D S P A M T X R B
What  food  and  drink  words  can  you  find
```

This is a brainteaser you have probably come across in puzzle magazines, but that doesn't make it any easier.

The words which are hidden in the screen spaghetti are all four letter — related to food or drink.

How to play

When you have found one of the twenty words on the screen, key it in and press RETURN.

If your guess is correct your word will be ticked. After a few seconds the word will be erased and your next word must be entered.

The words you have found to date will be coloured in red on the screen, which should make it easier for you to spot the others.

To change the screen key in NEXT and press RETURN.

The computer takes a short time to generate the letters before they are displayed, and during this time the screen is blank.

Programming hints

Two methods are used to reduce the memory required in this program. First, all the numerical arrays are integer arrays, this is shown by putting a % sign after the variable names. Secondly the possible words are stored one after another in a string, instead of an array.

You can alter the words that can be found if you wish. There are 57 of them in order to make the puzzles as random as possible. These words are stored in the variable W$ on line 80 to 120. If you can think of other four-letter words to do with food or drink, then just replace some of the words with those you have chosen. If you want to put in words on a different subject, then think of a subject and replace the words in W$ with your words all joined together. Remember there must be 57 of them, and they must all have four letters.

If you wish to use longer or shorter words, all words must still be of the same length as each other. Change the words in W$ so the total number of letters is still the same. Then change ID in line 310 so 4 is replaced by the number of letters in each word, and 57 is replaced by the maximum number of words in W$. The minimum value of ID must be 1 so 3 should be changed accordingly. The 4 in line 350 should also be changed. If the word length is increased more elements of array L$ must be checked to be empty and then assigned a letter in lines 360 to 450. Also the 80 (which is 20 words of 4 letters) and 4 in line 680 should be changed. The 4 in line 690, and the 3 and 4 in line 730 should also be changed.

Special feature

If you wish to have a collection of word search puzzles to be completed away from the computer, and you have a 40 column printer, then if you direct output to the printer, the puzzles will be printed out for you.

Program

```
10 REM WORD-SEARCH
20 REM COPYRIGHT (C) G.LUDINSKI 1983
30 POKE53280,2:POKE53281,12:REM BORDER A
ND BACKGROUND
40 POKE53272,23:REM LOWER CASE
50 DIML$(24,18),CH%(20,14),P%(20)
60 HO$=CHR$(19):CL$=CHR$(147):CG$=CHR$(1
51):CU$=CHR$(145)
70 PRINTCG$;CL$;
80 W$="FISHMEATCAKESOUPPEASSALTCHOPCORNW
INEBEERLIMEBRANBEANVEALROLLHAKEPIKEROC"
90 W$=W$+"KSPAMMALTROLL"
100 W$=W$+"MINTLAMBPORKBEEFTARTCANENUTST
UNARICESAKISAGOLOAFGAMEHERBPEARMILKLARD"
110 W$=W$+"CHIPSTEW"
120 W$=W$+"OATSPATESAGEMACECRABMASHCOLAP
ITHPEELSOYALEEKDUCKDILLYOLKBALMSUETSODA"
130 DEF FNRN(A)=INT(RND(1)*A+1)
140 S$="                   "
150 P%(0)=240
160 REM
170 REM GENERATE LETTERS
180 REM
```

```
190 PRINTCL$;
200 WC$=""
210 FORI=1TO14
220 FORJ=1TO20
230 L$(J,I)=""
240 CH%(J,I)=0
250 NEXTJ
260 NEXTI
270 FORI=1TO20
280 D=FNRN(3)
290 R=FNRN(10):IFD=2THENR=FNRN(14)
300 C=FNRN(16):IFD=1THENC=FNRN(20)
310 ID=4*FNRN(57)-3
320 FORQ=0TOI-1:IFID=P%(Q)THENGOTO310
330 NEXTQ
340 P%(I)=ID
350 WD$=MID$(W$,ID,4)
360 IFD=1ANDL$(C,R)=""ANDL$(C,R+1)=""AND
L$(C,R+2)=""ANDL$(C,R+3)=""THENGOTO380
370 GOTO390
380 FORK=0TO3:L$(C,R+K)=MID$(WD$,K+1,1):
CH%(C,R+K)=I:NEXTK:GOTO470
390 C1=C+1:C2=C+2:C3=C+3:R1=R+1
400 IFD=2ANDL$(C,R)=""ANDL$(C1,R)=""ANDL
$(C2,R)=""ANDL$(C3,R)=""THENGOTO420
410 GOTO430
420 FORK=0TO3:L$(C+K,R)=MID$(WD$,K+1,1):
CH%(C+K,R)=I:NEXTK:GOTO470
430 IFD=3ANDL$(C,R)=""ANDL$(C1,R1)=""AND
L$(C2,R+2)=""ANDL$(C3,R+3)=""THENGOTO450
440 GOTO280
450 FORK=0TO3:L$(C+K,R+K)=MID$(WD$,K+1,1
):CH%(C+K,R+K)=I:NEXTK:GOTO470
460 GOTO280
470 WC$=WC$+WD$
480 NEXTI
490 REM
500 REM DISPLAY LETTERS
510 REM
520 PRINTHO$
530 FORI=1TO14
540 FORJ=1TO20
```

```
550 IFL$(J,I)=""THENPRINTTAB(2*J-2);CHR$
(64+FNRN(26));" ";:GOTO570
560 PRINTTAB(2*J-2);L$(J,I);" ";
570 NEXTJ
580 NEXTI
590 FORJ=1TO7:PRINT:NEXT
600 REM
610 REM CHECK ANSWER
620 REM
630 FORN=1TO20
640 XT=0:YT=20:P$="WHAT FOOD AND DRINK W
ORDS CAN YOU FIND "+S$:GOSUB830
650 PRINTCU$;CU$
660 INPUTI$
670 IFI$="NEXT"THENGOTO190
680 FORM=1TO80STEP4
690 IFI$<>MID$(WC$,M,4)THENGOTO770
700 YT=21:XT=8:P$="⌐":GOSUB830
710 FORI=1TO14
720 FORJ=1TO20
730 IFCH%(J,I)=(M+3)/4THENXT=2*J-2:YT=I:
GOSUB800
740 NEXTJ
750 NEXTI
760 GOTO790
770 NEXTM
780 GOTO640
790 NEXTN
800 REM COLOUR LETTER SUBROUTINE
810 POKE55296+(YT*40)+XT,2
820 RETURN
830 REM POKE IN PROMPT SUBROUTINE
840 FORF=XTTOXT+LEN(P$)-1
850 SD=(40*YT)+F
860 POKE55296+SD,11
870 CC$=MID$(P$,F-XT+1,1):IFCC$=" "THENP
OKE1024+SD,32:GOTO890
880 POKE1024+SD,ASC(CC$)-64
890 NEXTF
900 RETURN
```

FRACTIONS AND PERCENTAGES

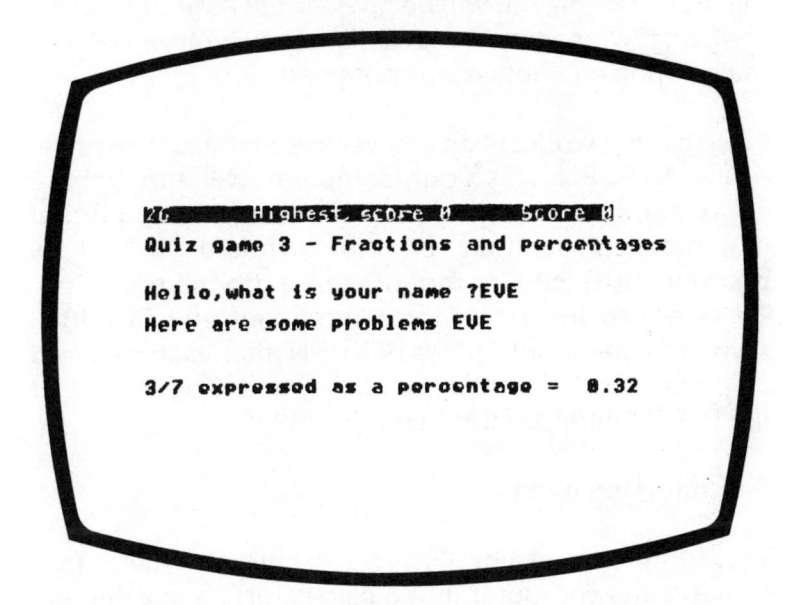

```
26        Highest score 0        Score 0
Quiz game 3 - Fractions and percentages

Hello,what is your name ?EVE
Here are some problems EVE

3/7 expressed as a percentage =   0.32
```

If you have trouble converting percentages to fractions and vice versa then this is for you.

How to play

You will be given five minutes to answer as many questions as possible, and you may press P and RETURN for pass if you cannot work out an answer.

You will not be penalised for 'passes'.

At the end of five minutes, or sooner if you enter N for NO in answer to the question "do you want any more", your score sheet showing tries, correct answers and average time per answer will appear. If you wish to proceed, then press Y and RETURN and the program will continue to ask you questions.

You can have two tries at each question if you wish. After the first attempt, you will be given a hint as to the correct answer. If your second answer is wrong, you will be told the solution and how it was obtained.

If you cannot work out an answer in your head then press ? and RETURN and your computer will turn into a calculator and you can then use the normal mathematical symbols on the keyboard as well as brackets, SQR (square root of) and ↑ (to the power of). To return to the main game type cont and RETURN. Always remember to press RETURN after each required response. For example to add 2 and 3 type 2 + 3 (RETURN), then cont (RETURN).

Programming hints

The subroutine at line 640 is a useful subroutine that converts the computer into a calculator. It uses the fact that if you PRINT an Arithmetic expression and then press RETURN in immediate mode (i.e. not within a program) then the answer will be displayed. For example, if you key in 'PRINT 3☐2' then press RETURN the answer 5 is displayed.

The conversion from fraction to percentage routine expects the percentage value to be entered to two places of decimals i.e. it expects the player to key in 66.66 not 66.7. If the programmer requires more or fewer decimal places, then A$ should be changed accordingly. The trick to write a number to a certain number of decimal places is to multiply it by 10 to the power of the number of decimal places you require, then find the integral part, then divide by the same number. In the program the fraction F/G is multiplied by a further 10 0 before conversion as the number is a percentage.

Even though the answer is given to a certain number of decimal places any answer, provided it is within 1 of the correct answer is accepted. This is so that the answer is marked correct however inaccurate the method used to obtain it. The most accurate method is to use the calculator routine provided but players may prefer to use mental arithmetic for speed.

Program

```
0 GOTO10
1 STOP:RETURN
10 REM FRACTIONS AND PERCENTAGES QUIZ
20 REM COPYRIGHT (C) G.LUDINSKI 1983
30 S$="                    "
40 DEF FNS(Y)=LEN(STR$(Y))-SGN(SGN(Y)+1)
50 CL$=CHR$(147):R1$=CHR$(18):R0$=CHR$(146):CG$=CHR$(151):C1$=CHR$(31)
60 HO$=CHR$(19):YE$=CHR$(158):S1=54273:S2=54272:RD$=CHR$(28):CU$=CHR$(145)
70 CD$=CHR$(17):CN$=" ES,CONGRATULATIONS "
80 DIMS%(5,3)
90 POKE53280,2:POKE53281,12:POKE53272,23:REM BORDER,BACKGROUND AND LOWER CASE
92 PRINTCG$;
100 PRINTCL$:PRINTR1$;S$;:PRINT"       RACTIONS AND PERCENTAGES QUIZ       ";S$;R0$
110 GOSUB1050:REM READ TUNE
120 TI$="000000"
130 INPUT" ELLO,WHAT IS YOUR NAME ";NAM$
140 PRINT:PRINT" ERE ARE SOME PROBLEMS ";:IFNAM$<>"NO SOUND"THENPRINTNAM$:GOTO160
150 PRINT
160 W=1:C=0:T=1:FORP=1TO5:GOSUB350
170 PRINT:PRINTQ$" = ";:GOSUB880
180 IFI$="?"THENGOSUB640
190 CT=0:FORJ=1TOLEN(I$):II$=MID$(I$,J,1):IFASC(II$)>47ANDASC(II$)<58THENCT=1
```

```
200 IFX<9ANDCT=1AND(II$="+"ORII$="-"ORII
$="*"ORII$="/")THENGOTO270
210 NEXT
220 IFX=9AND I$=A$THENGOTO250
230 IFX<9ANDABS(VAL(I$)-A)<=XTHENGOTO250
240 GOTO270
250 PRINT:PRINTYE$;CN$;CG$:C=C+1:PRINT:I
FNAM$="NO SOUND"THENGOTO300
260 GOSUB970:GOTO300
270 IFT=1THENPRINT:PRINTC1$;"/O,";H$;",T
RY AGAIN";CG$:T=2:GOTO170
280 PRINT:PRINTRD$;"♥ORRY,THE ANSWER =":
PRINT:PRINTL$:PRINT:PRINTM$
290 PRINT:PRINTN$;CG$
300 IFP=5THENPRINT:PRINT" IOUR SCORE = "C
*20"%":PRINT
310 PRINT:INPUT"─O YOU WANT MORE ? (Y/N)
 ";R$:PRINT
320 IFR$<>"Y"ANDR$<>"N"ANDR$<>""THENGOTO
310
330 IFR$="Y"ORR$=""THENT=1:PRINTCL$:NEXT
P:C=0:GOTO160
340 GOTO630
350 L$="":M$="":N$="":FORJ=1TO10:A$(J)="
":NEXTJ:B=40
360 W=-W:F=INT(RND(2)*9+1):N=1
370 G=INT(RND(3)*9+1):J1=INT(RND(4)*19+1
)
380 GOSUB1100
390 IFF=GORF/G=INT(F/G)ORG/F=INT(G/F)THE
NGOTO360
400 IFF<GTHENE=INT(F*10000/G)/100:J=J1*5
410 IFG<FTHENE=INT(G*10000/F)/100:H=G:G=
F:F=H:J=J1*2
420 E$=RIGHT$(STR$(E),FNS(E)):F$=RIGHT$(
STR$(F),FNS(F))
430 G$=RIGHT$(STR$(G),FNS(G)):J$=RIGHT$(
STR$(J),FNS(J))
440 IFW=1THENGOTO550
450 X=9
460 Q$=J$+" PERCENT CONVERTED INTO A FRA
CTION "
```

```
470 H$="P PERCENT IS P/100.┐F TOP AND BO
TTOM OF FRACTION ARE EXACTLY DIVISIBLE"
480 H$=H$+" BY THESAME NUMBERS THEN DIVI
DE BY THESE       NUMBERS"
490 HU=100:FORI=1TO8
500 IFJ/5=INT(J/5)ANDHU/5=INT(HU/5)THENJ
=J/5:HU=HU/5
510 IFJ/2=INT(J/2)ANDHU/2=INT(HU/2)THENJ
=J/2:HU=HU/2
520 NEXTI:A$=RIGHT$(STR$(J),FNS(J))   +"/
"+RIGHT$(STR$(HU),FNS(HU))
530 L$=A$
540 M$="AS "+J$+"/100 = "+A$
550 IFW=-1THENGOTO620
560 X=1
570 Q$=F$+"/"+G$+" EXPRESSED AS A PERCEN
TAGE "
580 H$="P/Q IS (P/Q) X 100 PERCENT"
590 A=E
600 A$=E$:L$=A$+" PERCENT"
610 M$="AS ("+F$+"/"+G$+") X 100 = "+E$
620 RETURN
630 END
640 REM CALCULATOR SUBROUTINE
650 GOSUB760
660 IFVP>14THENFORI=1TO9:PRINTCD$;:NEXT
670 PRINTHO$;:FORI=1TO15:PRINTCD$;:NEXT
680 PRINTR1$;C1$;"─ALCULATOR MODE (TYPE
CONT TO CONTINUE)";CG$;
690 FORD=1664TO2023:POKED,32:NEXT
700 POKE631,63:POKE198,1:GOSUB1
710 FORD=1624TO2023:POKED,32:NEXT
720 PRINTHO$;:IFVP>14THENFORI=1TO15:PRIN
TCD$;:NEXT:GOTO740
730 FORI=1TOVP+1:PRINTCD$;:NEXT
740 GOSUB880
750 RETURN
760 REM CURSOR Y POSITION SUBROUTINE
770 FORGG=1984TO1024STEP-40
780 IFPEEK(GG)<>32THENVP=INT((GG-1024)/4
0):GOTO800
790 NEXT
```

```
800 RETURN
810 REM POKE SCREEN SUBROUTINE
820 FORFF=XTTOXT+LEN(P$)-1
830 SD=(40*YT)+FF
840 POKE55296+SD,11
850 CC$=MID$(P$,FF-XT+1,1):POKE1024+SD,A
SC(CC$):GOTO860
860 NEXT
870 RETURN
880 REM KEY IN SUBROUTINE
890 POKE198,0
900 GETI$:P$=LEFT$(STR$(INT(TI/60))+" SE
C"+S$,39)
910 IFI$=""THENXT=0:YT=0:GOSUB810:GOTO90
0
920 IFI$<>""THENPRINTI$;:GOTO930
930 GETI2$:IFI2$=""THENGOTO930
940 IFI2$<>CHR$(13)THENPRINTI2$;:I$=I$+I
2$:GOTO930
950 PRINT
960 RETURN
970 REM SOUND SUBROUTINE
980 POKE54296,15:POKE54277,190:POKE54278
,248:POKE54276,17
990 FORH=1TO5
1000 POKES1,S%(H,1):POKES2,S%(H,2)
1010 FORTT=1TOS%(H,3):NEXT
1020 NEXT
1030 POKE54276,0:POKE54277,0:POKE54278,0
1040 RETURN
1050 REM READ TUNE SUBROUTINE
1060 RESTORE
1070 FORH=1TO5:READS%(H,1),S%(H,2),S%(H,
3):NEXT
1080 DATA 38,126,200,43,52,200,48,127,20
0,51,97,400,38,126,400
1090 RETURN
1100 REM TAKE OUT FACTORS SUBROUTINE
1110 FORI=2TO3
1120 IFE/I=INT(E/I)ANDF/I=INT(F/I)THENE=
E/I:F=F/I:GOTO1120
1130 NEXT
1140 RETURN
```

FRANCIS DRAKE ADVENTURE GAME

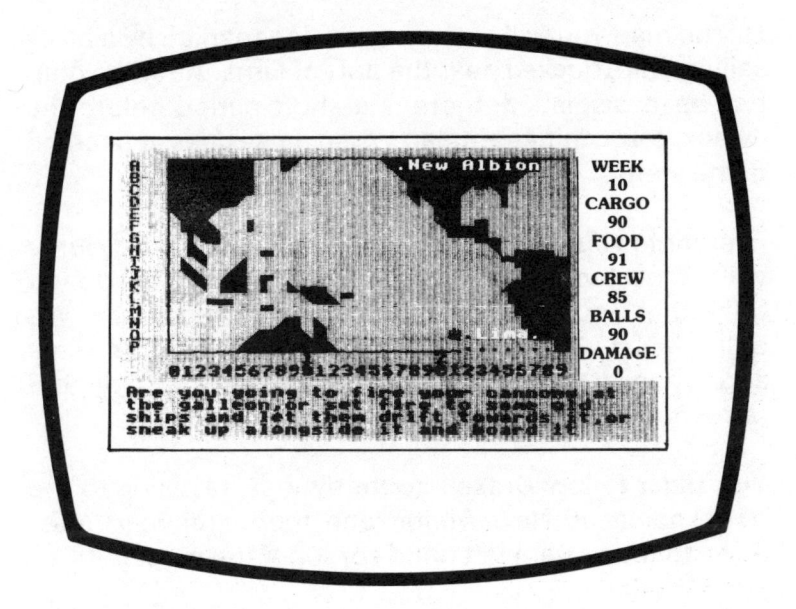

This is by far and away the most ambitious, interesting and testing program in this book.

This is an authentic historical adventure game based on Francis Drake's circumnavigation of the world, from 1577 to 1580. As you travel in the footsteps of the greatest of Elizabeth the First's free-booting adventurers, you will encounter the same problems and challenges as Drake.

Drake sailed in search of the elusive North West Passage that would allow him access to the Pacific, and the galleons of the Spanish Empire. As history books will already have told you, he did not find the object of his quest, but he did find much more, and so will you as you sail into the Francis Adventure Game.

How to play

When the program has been loaded and RUN, you will hear the gentle lapping of waves against the shore.

On the map you will see your position marked by a black sailing ship, docked near the port of Lima. After the map has been displayed, there is a short period before the "week, cargo" titles appear. When these titles appear the game starts.

Everytime you use this game, the dangers and treasures will be located in different parts of the ocean, so do not think that you can predict your moves too easily. We didn't feel it was fair, however, to move the rocks, reefs and Spanish galleons during the game, so try and remember their locations. It will help you considerably.

You **must** follow Drake's route by first travelling to the port known as New Albion and thence onward, past Java, to the bottom left hand corner of the map.

Your aim is to reach the bottom of the map with, at least, four times the amount of the cargo with which you began.

If you achieve this feat of daring then you will, naturally, be rewarded by the gift of a knighthood from your grateful, and avaricious, Queen.

You move using the ARROW cursor keys.

At intervals you will be told the situation at sea and asked which action you would like to take, from the choice shown.

Remember to consider your options carefully as to the amounts of cargo, food, cannon balls and crew conditions.

If the program does not understand your response, you will hear a two-note tune and you should try again.

Damage rating is based on a 1 to 10 scale. If you are damaged to the level of 10 then I'm afraid that it's into the sea for you, as the Golden Hind settles gently below your feet.

Do your best, as the present Government is emptying the coffers more quickly than you are filling them.

Hints and changes you can make

One of the problems of displaying a map on the screen, is how to reduce the memory required and the number of lines needed to describe the map. This is done here by defining a string array M$, with the number of elements being equal to the number of rows on the map. Standard shapes are then used. The shapes are as shown below:

■ ▬ ◧ ◨ ◸ ◤ ◥ ◣ ■
1   2   3   4   5   6   7   8   9

Each row of the map is assigned to an element of M$ using the above shapes, and zero (to represent blanks).

If you find the adventure too easy, then reduce the cargo (CA), food (SU), crew (CR), and/or cannon balls (BA) that you start with. They are on line 440. If you find that knighthood escapes you, then reduce the 400 in line 560.

Program

```
10 REM FRANCIS DRAKE ADVENTURE GAME
20 REM COPYRIGHT (C) G.LUDINSKI 1983
30 DIMM$(17)
40 DEF FNRN(MAX)=INT(RND(1)*MAX+1)
```

```
50 S$="                            "
60 AL=0
70 WH$=CHR$(5):CL$=CHR$(147):HO$=CHR$(19
):CU$=CHR$(145):BL$=CHR$(144)
80 LB$=CHR$(154):CD$=CHR$(17):R1$=CHR$(1
8):R0$=CHR$(146):YE$=CHR$(158)
90 BU$=CHR$(31):GR$=CHR$(30)
100 XP=782:YP=781:XY=65520
110 S1=54273:S2=54272:VL=54296:WV=54276:
AD=54277:SR=54278:REM SOUND VARIABLES
120 SH$="&"
130 LA$=CHR$(157):RA$=CHR$(29):DA$=CHR$(
17):UA$=CHR$(145)
140 M$(1)=" 99999930450000079999999990
00 "
150 M$(2)=" 99999930000000000799999999950
00 "
160 M$(3)=" 999999300600000000009999517300
00 "
170 M$(4)=" 99999500000000000007799000300
00 "
180 M$(5)=" 79950000000000000000099000000
00 "
190 M$(6)=" 09980030000000000000079290000
00 "
200 M$(7)=" 04790000000000000000001192000
00 "
210 M$(8)=" 04800002000000000000000007022
20 "
220 M$(9)=" 08700600000000000000000000199
99 "
230 M$(10)=" 07806902000000000000000000004
999 "
240 M$(11)=" 00709903082200000000000000009
999 "
250 M$(12)=" 00022000007981000000000000009
999 "
260 M$(13)=" 00000001000000000000000000009
999 "
270 M$(14)=" 00000000690800000000000000004
999 "
```

```
280 M$(15)=" 000000699989000000000000000
999 "
290 M$(16)=" 000006999999800000000000000
099 "
300 GOSUB2520
310 GOSUB2250
320 M$(15)=" 000000699989000000000000000E
EEE "
330 M$(16)=" 000006999999800000000000000E
EEE "
340 GOSUB1180
350 FORY=1TO16
360 FORX=2TO31
370 C$=MID$(M$(Y),X,1)
380 IFC$="9"THENGOTO430
390 IFC$="0"THENIS=INT(7*RND(1)):GOSUB19
50:GOTO430
400 IFC$="E"THENIS=4:GOSUB1950:GOTO430
410 IF(X>4ANDX<15ANDY>7ANDY<14)THENIS=IN
T(2*RND(1)+7):GOSUB1950:GOTO430
420 IS=10:GOSUB1950
430 NEXT:NEXT
440 CA=100:SU=100:CR=85:BA=100:DA=0:WK=1
450 EN=0:AL=0
460 X=29:Y=16:X1=29:Y1=16
470 IFWK=1THENPOKEXP,X+4:POKEYP,Y:SYSXY:
PRINTBL$;SH$;WH$;
480 POKEXP,35:POKEYP,0:SYSXY:PRINTLB$;"W
EEK"
490 POKEYP,3:SYSXY:PRINT"CARGO"
500 POKEYP,6:SYSXY:PRINT"FOOD":POKEYP,9:
SYSXY:PRINT"CREW":POKEYP,12:SYSXY:PRINT"
BALLS"
510 POKEYP,15:SYSXY:PRINT"DAMG.";WH$
520 IFX<>10RY<>16THENGOTO580
530 GOSUB1180:PRINT"YOU HAVE SURVIVED TH
E UNKNOWN,AND NOW   K OW ";
540 PRINT"YOU ARE THE FIRST COMMANDER OF
  A   FLEET TO SAIL AROUND THE WORLD."
550 EN=1
560 IFCA>=400THENPRINT"ARISE SIR FRANCIS
"
```

```
570 GOTO2240
580 IF(X=17ANDY=1)OR(X=18ANDY=2)OR(X=19A
ND Y=4)THENAL=1
590 IFX<15ANDAL=0THENGOSUB1180:PRINT"GO
BACK TO NEW ALBION"
600 IFSU>0THENGOTO640
610 GOSUB1180
620 PRINT"YOUR SUPPLIES HAVE BEEN USED U
P SO YOUR ";
630 PRINT"CREW MUTINIES ,AND KILLS YOU":
SU=0:EN=1
640 IFCR>0THENGOTO680
650 GOSUB1180:PRINT"YOUR CREW HAVE ALL B
EEN KILLED IN BATTLEOR ";
660 PRINT"HAVE DIED OF SCURVY,TYPHUS OR
        DYSENTERY.YOU ARE STRANDED";
670 PRINT" WITHOUTTHEM,":CR=0:EN=1
680 IFDA>10THENGOSUB1180:PRINT"YOUR SHIP
 HAS FILLED WITH WATER AND SUNK":EN=1
690 IFBA<0THENBA=0
700 IFCA<0THENCA=0
710 IFEN=1THENGOTO2240
720 POKEXP,36:POKEYP,1:SYSXY:PRINTRIGHT$
(" "+STR$(WK),4)
730 POKEYP,4:SYSXY:PRINTRIGHT$("    "+STR
$(CA),4)
740 POKEXP,36:POKEYP,7:SYSXY:PRINTRIGHT$
("    "+STR$(SU),4)
750 POKEYP,10:SYSXY:PRINTRIGHT$("    "+ST
R$(CR),4)
760 POKEXP,36:POKEYP,13:SYSXY:PRINTRIGHT
$("      "+STR$(BA),4)
770 POKEXP,36:POKEYP,16:SYSXY:PRINTRIGHT
$("      "+STR$(DA),4)
780 GETI$:IFI$=""THENGOTO780
790 IF(X=1ANDI$=LA$)OR(X=30ANDI$=RA$)OR(
Y=1ANDI$=UA$)OR(Y=16ANDI$=DA$)THENGOTO78
0
800 GOSUB1180
810 XM$=MID$(M$(Y),X-1,1):X0$=MID$(M$(Y)
,X,1):XP$=MID$(M$(Y),X+1,1)
```

```
820 YM$=MID$(M$(Y-1),X,1):YP$=MID$(M$(Y+
1),X,1)
830 IFI$=LA$ANDXM$<>"0"ANDXM$<>"9"ANDX0$
<>"2"THENX=X-1
840 IFI$=RA$AND(XP$<>"2"ANDXP$<>"9"ANDXO
$<>"0")THENX=X+1
850 IFI$=DA$AND(YP$<>"3"ANDYP$<>"9"ANDX0
$<>"1")THENY=Y+1
860 IFI$=UA$AND(YM$<>"1"ANDYM$<>"9"ANDX0
$<>"3")THENY=Y-1
870 WK=WK+1
880 IFDA<>0THENDA=DA+1
890 SU=SU-1
900 POKEXP,X1+4:POKEYP,Y1:SYSXY:PRINT"."
;
910 POKEXP,X+4:POKEYP,Y:SYSXY:PRINTBL$;S
H$;WH$;
920 IFX0$<>"A"ORDA=0THENGOTO950
930 DA=0:GOSUB1180:PRINT;"YOU HAVE ";
940 PRINT"ARRIVED AT A PORT SO YOU CAN
 NOW GET YOUR SHIP REPAIRED":GOTO1010
950 IFX=X1ANDY=Y1ANDWK<>1THENGOSUB2010:G
OSUB1030:GOTO1010
960 IFX0$="4"THENGOSUB1180:GOTO1010
970 IFX0$="5"THENGOSUB1220
980 IFX0$="6"THENGOSUB1430
990 IFX0$="7"THENGOSUB1860
1000 IFX0$="8"THENGOSUB1910
1010 X1=X:Y1=Y
1020 GOTO520
1030 REM REEF SUBROUTINE
1040 W=INT(2*RND(1))
1050 RR$="ROCK":IFX<15THENRR$="REEF"
1060 IFW=0THENGOSUB1180:PRINT"THERE IS A
 ";RR$;" AHEAD.TURN AROUND":GOTO1170
1070 GOSUB1180:PRINT"YOU HAVE RUN AGROUN
D ON A ";RR$;".ARE YOU  GOING TO THROW "
;
1080 PRINT"CARGO AND GUNS OVERBOARD,OR P
UT OUT AN ANCHOR TO WINDWARD"
1090 INPUTR$:SG$="OVERBOARD":GOSUB2060:I
FFO=1THENR$="OVERBOARD":GOTO1120
```

```
1100 SG$="ANCHOR":GOSUB2060:IFFO=1THENR$
="ANCHOR":GOTO1120
1110 PRINTCU$;:GOSUB2130:GOTO1090
1120 IFR$="OVERBOARD"THENCA=CA-FNRN(20):
GOTO1170
1130 W2=INT(2*RND(1)):GOSUB1180
1140 IFW2=0THENPRINT"YOU HAVE BROKEN FRE
E WITHOUT ANY        SIGNIFICANT DAMAGE"
1150 IF W2<>0THENPRINT"YOUR SHIP,THE GOL
DEN HIND,IS HOLED.     ";
1160 IFW2<>0THENPRINT"RETURN TO DRY LAND
 AT ONCE OR IT WILL    SINK":DA=DA+1
1170 RETURN
1180 REM   BLANK LINES
1190 POKEXP,0:POKEYP,19:SYSXY:PRINTS$;S$
;S$;S$;LEFT$(S$,39);
1200 POKEXP,0:POKEYP,19:SYSXY
1210 RETURN
1220 REM NAMED SHIP SUBROUTINE
1230 GOSUB2190:GOSUB1180
1240 M1$="YOU SEE A SPANISH GALLEON,THE
CACAFUEGO.ARE YOU GOING TO ATTACK IT OR"
1250 M1$=M1$+" IGNORE IT"
1260 M2$="YOU SEE A SPANISH GALLEON,THE
ESPRITO    SANTO.ARE YOU GOING TO ATTACK"
1270 M2$=M2$+" IT OR       IGNORE IT"
1280 IFFNRN(2)=1THENPRINTM1$:GOTO1300
1290 PRINTM2$
1300 INPUTR$:SG$="ATTACK":GOSUB2060:IFFO
=1THENR$="ATTACK":GOTO1330
1310 SG$="IGNORE":GOSUB2060:IFFO=1THENR$
="IGNORE":PRINTCU$;:GOTO1330
1320 PRINTCU$;:GOSUB2130:GOTO1300
1330 IFR$<>"ATTACK"THENGOTO1420
1340 GOSUB1180
1350 IFCA>0THENGOTO1390
1360 PRINT"YOU DRAW ALONGSIDE THE GALLEO
N THEN FIND YOU HAVE NO ";
1370 PRINT"CANNON BALLS LEFT SO    THE SP
ANISH WIN THE BATTLE AND LEAVE YOU TO DI
E"
```

```
1380 EN=1:GOTO1420
1390 PRINT"YOU FIGHT A FIERCE BATTLE AND
 FINALLY    TAKE COMMAND OF THE GALLEON";
1400 PRINT" AND TRANSFERITS CARGO TO THE
 HOLD OF THE GOLDEN HIND"
1410 CA=CA+FNRN(20):BA=BA-FNRN(20):FORD=
1TO100:NEXTD
1420 RETURN
1430 REM SHIP SUBROUTINE
1440 GOSUB2190:GOSUB1180
1450 PRINT"YOU SEE A SPANISH GALLEON.ARE
 YOU GOING TO ATTACK IT OR IGNORE IT"
1460 INPUTR$:SG$="ATTACK":GOSUB2060:IFFO
=1THENR$="ATTACK":GOTO1490
1470 SG$="IGNORE":GOSUB2060:IFFO=1THENR$
="IGNORE":GOTO1490
1480 PRINTCU$;:GOSUB2130:GOTO1460
1490 IFR$="IGNORE"THENRETURN
1500 GOSUB1180
1510 PRINT"ARE YOU GOING TO FIRE YOUR CA
NNONS AT    THE GALLEON,OR SET FIRE TO ";
1520 PRINT" SOME OLD      SHIPS AND LET TH
EM DRIFT TOWARDS IT,OR   SNEAK UP ";
1530 PRINT"ALONGSIDE IT AND BOARD IT"
1540 INPUTR$:SG$="CANNON":GOSUB2060:IFFO
=1THENR$="CANNONS":GOTO1580
1550 SG$="SET FIRE":GOSUB2060:IFFO=1THEN
R$="SET FIRE":GOTO1580
1560 SG$="SNEAK":GOSUB2060:IFFO=1THENR$=
"SNEAK":GOTO1580
1570 PRINTCU$;:GOSUB2130:GOTO1540
1580 GOSUB1180
1590 IFR$<>"CANNONS"THENGOTO1660
1600 IFFNRN(2)=1THENGOTO1630
1610 PRINT"YOUR SHIP GETS HOLED AND SOME
 OF YOUR    CREW ARE SHOT.RETURN TO ";
1620 PRINT"DRY LAND AT ONCE":DA=DA+1:BA=
BA-FNRN(20):CR=CR-FNRN(10):GOTO1660
1630 PRINT"AS YOUR SHIP IS SMALLER AND L
OWER THAN    THE GALLEON,YOU MANAGE TO ";
1640 PRINT"PUT IT OUT OF ACTION AND BOAR
```

```
D IT,WITHOUT INCURRING     ANY DAMAGE TO Y
OUR";
1650 PRINT" SHIP.":CA=CA+FNRN(20):SU=SU+
FNRN(20):BA=BA+FNRN(20)
1660 IFR$<>"SET FIRE"THENGOTO1760
1670 GOSUB1180
1680 IFFNRN(2)THENGOTO1730
1690 PRINT"THE WIND CHANGES DIRECTION AN
D THE      BURNING SHIPS DRIFT TOWARDS";
1700 PRINT" THE GOLDEN HIND SETTING THE
MIZZEN MAST ALIGHT.    RETURN TO DRY ";
1710 PRINT"LAND AT ONCE"
1720 DA=DA+1:GOTO1760
1730 PRINT"THE BURNING SHIPS DRIFT TOWAR
DS THE     GALLEON SETTING IT ALIGHT.";
1740 PRINT"THE CAPTAIN    SURRENDERS AND
YOU TRANSFER HIS CARGO TOYOUR HOLD"
1750 CA=CA+FNRN(20):SU=SU+FNRN(20):BA=BA
+FNRN(20):GOTO1760
1760 IFR$<>"SNEAK"THENGOTO1850
1770 GOSUB1180
1780 IFFNRN(2)=1THENGOTO1820
1790 PRINT"THEY SEE YOU APPROACHING AND
REALISING   THAT YOU ARE ENGLISH THEY ";
1800 PRINT"OPEN FIRE,     SHOOTING SOME O
F YOUR CREW AND DAMAGING YOUR BOAT.RETUR
N";
1810 PRINT" TO PORT AT ONCE":BA=BA-FNRN(
20):DA=DA+1:CR=CR-FNRN(10):GOTO1850
1820 PRINT"THEY ASSUME YOU ARE SPANISH A
S ENGLISH   SHIPS HAVE NEVER BEEN THIS ";
1830 PRINT"FAR BEFORE,    SO YOU MANAGE TO
 BOARD THE GALLEON AND   CAPTURE IT AND I
TS";
1840 PRINT" RICH CARGO":CA=CA+FNRN(20):S
U=SU+FNRN(20):BA=BA+FNRN(20)
1850 RETURN
1860 REM TRADE SUBROUTINE
1870 GOSUB2190
1880 GOSUB1180:PRINT"YOU BUY CLOVES CHEA
PLY FROM THE           ISLANDERS"
1890 CA=CA+FNRN(20):SU=SU+FNRN(20)
```

```
1900 RETURN
1910 REM HOSTILE SUBROUTINE
1920 GOSUB2190
1930 GOSUB1180:PRINT"HOSTILE ISLANDERS P
ELT YOU WITH STONES":CR=CR-FNRN(20)
1940 RETURN
1950 REM INSERT SUBROUTINE
1960 IL$=RIGHT$(STR$(IS),LEN(STR$(IS))-1
)
1970 IFIS<>10THENM$(Y)=LEFT$(M$(Y),X-1)+
IL$+RIGHT$(M$(Y),31-X):GOTO1990
1980 M$(Y)=LEFT$(M$(Y),X-1)+"A"+RIGHT$(M
$(Y),31-X)
1990 RETURN
2000 POKE52,48:POKE56,48:CLR
2010 REM REEF COLLISION NOISE SUBROUTINE
2020 POKEWV,129:POKEVL,15:POKEAD,15:POKE
SR,248
2030 POKES1,68:POKES2,149:FORT=1TO200:NE
XTT
2040 POKEWV,0:POKEVL,0:POKEAD,0
2050 RETURN
2060 REM STRING IN STRING SUBROUTINE
2070 IFLEN(R$)<LEN(SG$)THENFO=0:GOTO2120
2080 FORL=1TOLEN(R$)-LEN(SG$)+1
2090 IFSG$=MID$(R$,L,LEN(SG$))THENFO=1:G
OTO2120
2100 NEXT
2110 FO=0
2120 RETURN
2130 REM WRONG SOUND SUBROUTINE
2140 POKEWV,33:POKEVL,15:POKEAD,190
2150 POKES1,45:POKES2,198:FORT=1TO300:NE
XTT
2160 POKES1,43:POKES2,52:FORT=1TO300:NEX
TT
2170 POKEWV,0:POKEVL,0:POKEAD,0
2180 RETURN
2190 REM WARNING SOUND SUBROUTINE
2200 POKEWV,33:POKEVL,15:POKEAD,190
2210 POKES1,68:POKES2,149:FORT=1TO200:NE
XTT
```

```
2220 POKEWV,0:POKEVL,0:POKEAD,0
2230 RETURN
2240 END
2250 REM DRAW MAP SUBROUTINE
2260 POKE53280,6:POKE53281,6:POKE53272,2
1:REM BORDER,BACKGROUND AND UPPER CASE
2270 PRINTCL$;GR$;
2280 TP$="":BT$="":FORI=1TO30:TP$=TP$+CH
R$(163):BT$=BT$+CHR$(164):NEXT
2290 TP$=LEFT$(TP$,9)
2300 PRINT"        ";BT$:FORJ=1TO16:PRINT"
 ";CHR$(64+J);" ";CHR$(167);:FORI=2TO31
2310 P=VAL(MID$(M$(J),I,1)):IFP=0THENPRI
NT" ";:GOTO2410
2320 IFP=1THENPRINTR1$;CHR$(162);R0$;:GO
TO2410
2330 IFP=2THENPRINTCHR$(162);:GOTO2410
2340 IFP=3THENPRINTCHR$(161);:GOTO2410
2350 IFP=4THENPRINTR1$;CHR$(161);R0$;:GO
TO2410
2360 IFP=5THENPRINTCHR$(169);:GOTO2410
2370 IFP=6THENPRINTR1$;CHR$(169);R0$;:GO
TO2410
2380 IFP=7THENPRINTCHR$(127);:GOTO2410
2390 IFP=8THENPRINTR1$;CHR$(127);R0$;:GO
TO2410
2400 IFP=9THENPRINTR1$;" ";R0$;
2410 NEXT
2420 PRINTCHR$(165)
2430 NEXT
2440 POKEXP,12:POKEYP,1:SYSXY:PRINTBL$;"
NEW ALBION";GR$;R1$;".";BL$
2450 POKEXP,28:POKEYP,15:SYSXY:PRINT"LIM
A";GR$;R1$;"."
2460 POKEXP,5:POKEYP,13:SYSXY:PRINTBL$;"
JAVA"
2470 PRINTWH$;
2480 POKEXP,5:POKEYP,17:SYSXY
2490 PRINTGR$;CHR$(163);TP$;"1";TP$;"2";
TP$
2500 POKEXP,5:POKEYP,18:SYSXY:PRINT"0123
4567890123456689O123456789"
```

```
2510 RETURN
2520 REM TITLE SUBROUTINE
2530 POKE53280,2:POKE53281,2:POKE53272,2
1:REM BORDER,BACKGROUND AND UPPER CASE
2540 PRINTCL$;YE$;
2550 FORI=1TO14:PRINTCD$;:NEXTI
2560 PRINTSPC(13);"FRANCIS DRAKE":PRINT:
PRINTSPC(13);"ADVENTURE GAME"
2570 FORI=1TO12:PRINTCD$;:NEXT
2580 PRINTBL$;
2590 PRINT"     COPYRIGHT (C) G.LUDINSKI
 1983";
2600 POKEWV,129:POKEAD,255:POKESR,255
2610 FORI=1TO3
2620 POKEVL,15:POKES1,45:POKES2,198:FORT
=1TO100:NEXTT
2630 POKES1,68:POKES2,149:FORT=1TO300:NE
XTT
2640 POKES1,45:POKES2,198:FORT=1TO300:NE
XTT
2650 POKES1,32:POKES2,94:FORT=1TO300:NEX
TT
2660 POKEVL,2:POKES1,28:POKES2,214:FORT=
1TO300:NEXTT
2670 NEXT
2680 RETURN
```

A-MAZE-ING

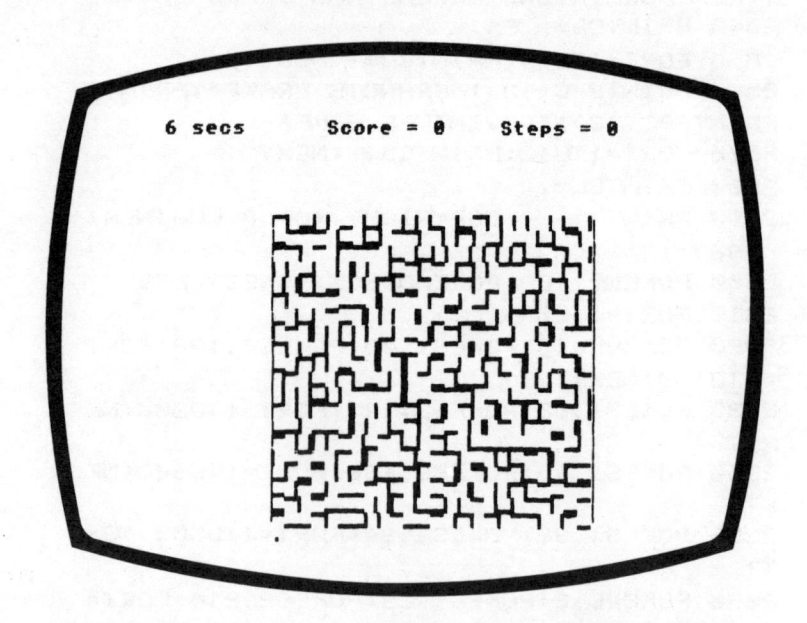

You are at the bottom of a complicated maze, and your objective is to reach the top in the quickest possible time, but also with the fewest number of moves possible.

Don't rush headlong into this one, as a little forward planning can save you time and points.

Every step counts as a point and every time you try to cross a barrier counts as a point.

You may exit the maze from any of the exits at the top.

How to play

You are represented by a dot in the lower left hand side of the maze, and you move by using the ARROW cursor keys.

Your score will be displayed at the top of the screen. The number of steps taken has a greater effect on your final score than the time factor.

You may, of course, retrace your steps and begin again from any point you wish to. When you reach the outside, a warbling sound will be heard and then a new maze is displayed.

We hope you make it, as there are plenty of other 'Brainteasers' waiting for you on the outside.

Programming hints

The maze is created of cells, each of which have one side blocked off. The cell shapes with dots in them are drawn using programmable graphics, the others are already defined.

You could increase the size of the maze by changing 20 and 24 in lines 220 and 240. The maze shown is 24 columns wide by 20 rows. The maze array M% must be DIMensioned 1 column and 2 rows larger than the actual array to allow for checking for the (X+1)th column and (Y+1)th row. If you want the maze in the centre of the screen you should change the PRINT statements in lines 210 and 230.

The start position of the dot in lines 280 and 290 would have to be changed. In a 20 row maze the 21st row is the row the dot starts on, so special conditions apply to this row in lines 350 to 440. If a different number of rows is chosen this 21 must be changed.

Program

```
10 REM A-MAZE-ING
20 REM COPYRIGHT (C) G.LUDINSKI 1983
30 POKE53280,2:POKE53281,2:POKE53272,21:
REM BORDER,BACKGROUND AND UPPER CASE
40 DIMM%(25,22),MZ(2,7)
50 HO$=CHR$(19):CL$=CHR$(147):WH$=CHR$(5
):RD$=CHR$(28)
60 CM=55296:PM=1024:KL=40:REM COLOUR AND
 SCREEN MAP
70 S1=54273:S2=54272:VL=54296:WV=54276:A
D=54277:SR=54278:REM SOUND VARIABLES
80 LA$=CHR$(157):RA$=CHR$(29):DA$=CHR$(1
7):UA$=CHR$(145)
90 MZ(1,0)=167:MZ(2,0)=103
100 MZ(1,1)=164:MZ(2,1)=100
110 MZ(1,2)=165:MZ(2,2)=101
120 MZ(1,3)=163:MZ(2,3)=99
130 Z$="00000001000000010000000100011001
000110010000000100000001000000001"
140 Y$="00000000000000000000000000011000
000110000000000000000000011111111"
150 W$="10000000100000001000000010011000
10011000100000001000000010000000"
160 R$="11111111000000000000000011000
0001100000000000000000000000000"
170 POKE53265,PEEK(53265)AND239
180 GOSUB490
190 POKE53265,PEEK(53265)OR16
200 PRINTCL$;WH$;
210 PRINT:PRINT
220 FORI=1TO20
230 PRINT:PRINT"           ";CHR$(MZ(1,0));
240 FORJ=1TO24
250 M%(J,I)=INT(RND(1)*4)
260 PRINTCHR$(MZ(1,M%(J,I)));
270 NEXT:PRINTCHR$(MZ(1,2));:NEXT
280 SE=0:X=1:Y=21:X1=1:Y1=21:TI$="000000
"
290 XX=X+7:YY=Y+2:C=46:GOSUB780
```

```
300 POKE198,0
310 SC=SE+INT(TI/300)
320 GETI$:IFI$=LA$ OR I$=RA$ OR I$=UA$ O
R I$=DA$THENGOTO350
330 PRINTHO$;STR$(INT(TI/60));" SECS";TA
B(12);"SCORE = ";STR$(SC);
340 PRINTTAB(25);"STEPS =";STR$(SE):GOTO
320
350 IF(X=1ANDI$=LA$)OR(X=24ANDI$=RA$)OR(
Y=1ANDI$=UA$)OR(Y=21ANDI$=DA$)THENGOTO31
0
360 IFI$=LA$AND((M%(X-1,Y)<>0ANDM%(X,Y)<
>2)ORY=21)THENX=X-1
370 IFI$=RA$AND((M%(X+1,Y)<>2ANDM%(X,Y)<
>0)ORY=21)THENX=X+1
380 IFI$=DA$AND((M%(X,Y+1)<>3ANDM%(X,Y)<
>1)ORY=21)THENY=Y+1
390 IFI$=UA$AND((M%(X,Y-1)<>1ANDM%(X,Y)<
>3)ORY=21)THENY=Y-1
400 SE=SE+1
410 IFY1=21THENXX=X1+7:YY=23:C=32:GOSUB7
80
420 IFY=21THENXX=X+7:YY=23:C=46:GOSUB780
430 IFY1<>21THENXX=X1+7:YY=Y1+2:C=MZ(2,M
%(X1,Y1)):GOSUB780
440 IFY<>21THENXX=X+7:YY=Y+2:C=MZ(2,M%(X
,Y)+4):GOSUB780
450 IFX=X1ANDY=Y1ANDSE<>0THENGOSUB820
460 IFY=1ANDM%(X,Y)<>3THENGOSUB880:GOTO2
00
470 X1=X:Y1=Y
480 GOTO310
490 REM DEFINE MAZE SHAPES SUBROUTINE
500 POKE56334,PEEK(56334)AND254:POKE1,PE
EK(1)AND251
510 C1=12288:C0=53248
520 FORI=0TO103
530 FORJ=0TO7
540 POKEC1+I*8+J,PEEK(C0+I*8+J)
550 NEXT
560 NEXT
570 POKE1,PEEK(1)OR4:POKE56334,PEEK(5633
4)OR1
```

```
580 POKE53272,(PEEK(53272)AND240)+12
590 CN=27:CC$=Z$:GOSUB640:MZ(2,4)=CN
600 CN=29:CC$=Y$:GOSUB640:MZ(2,5)=CN
610 CN=37:CC$=W$:GOSUB640:MZ(2,6)=CN
620 CN=38:CC$=R$:GOSUB640:MZ(2,7)=CN
630 RETURN
640 REM REDEFINE CHARACTER SUBROUTINE
650 CG=C1+(CN*8)
660 FORI=0TO7
670 N$=MID$(CC$,I*8+1,8)
680 GOSUB720
690 POKECG+I,TF
700 NEXT
710 RETURN
720 REM BINARY TO DECIMAL SUBROUTINE
730 TF=0
740 FORL=0TO7
750 TF=TF+(2↑L)*VAL(MID$(N$,8-L,1))
760 NEXT
770 RETURN
780 REM POKE TO SCREEN SUBROUTINE
790 SD=(KL*YY)+XX
800 POKECM+SD,1:POKEPM+SD,C
810 RETURN
820 REM WALL SOUND SUBROUTINE
830 POKEWV,129:POKEAD,170:POKEVL,15:POKE
SR,248
840 POKES1,68:POKES2,149
850 FORTT=1TO200:NEXTTT
860 POKEWV,0:POKEAD,0:POKEVL,0:POKESR,0
870 RETURN
880 REM ARCADE SOUND SUBROUTINE
890 POKEAD,144:POKESR,243
900 POKEWV,33
910 POKEVL,15
920 FORK=1TO20
930 POKES1,134:POKES2,30 :FORT=1TO100:NE
XT
940 POKES1,8:POKES2,97:FORT=1TO100:NEXT
950 NEXT
960 POKEWV,0:POKEVL,0:POKEAD,0:POKESR,0
970 RETURN
```

CLOSE ENCOUNTERS OF THE FOURTH KIND

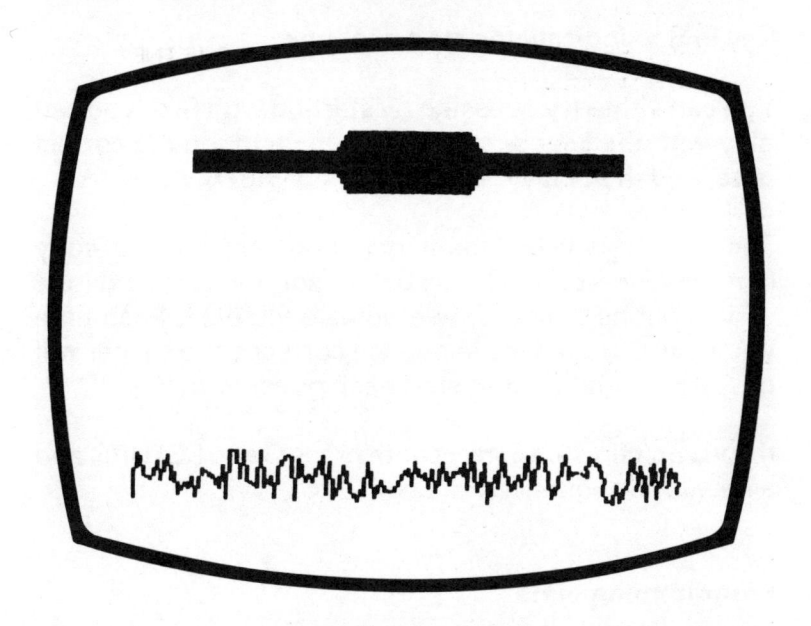

The aliens have sneaked into this book after all — but we believe they are friendly. It's up to you to find out.

Hovering above a field, lights rotating around it's outer edge, is a flying saucer. From the saucer comes a sequence of notes which may contain a message of peace. To find out you must repeat the notes in the same sequence as the aliens have transmitted them.

Every time you repeat the notes properly, the saucer will descend one level towards the ground. Try and bring them in carefully as the last time we succeeded the space vessel blew up after landing.

How to play

The number keys 1 to 8 represent a note in the octave starting with middle C.

Key in S to indicate the start of a tune.

You can either try guessing by starting with S, or you can play with the keyboard until you have found the correct note, and then play the tune starting with S.

The saucer will first emit one note and, if you copy correctly, descends slightly before sounding its next tone which will be a tune of two notes and so on. Each time you have guessed the sequence correctly the saucer will descend. Remember to start each guess with S.

If you can't find the correct note press G and RETURN and a new tune sequence will begin.

Programming hints

This uses a useful method of positioning text on the screen. The X position is POKEd into address 782 and the Y position into 781 then the machine code routine at 65520 is called.

You could decrease the number of possible notes in the tunes by changing the maximum value of N(L) in line 230.

Program

```
10 REM CLOSE ENCOUNTERS OF THE FOURTH KIND
20 REM COPYRIGHT (C) G.LUDINSKI 1983
30 POKE53280,2:POKE53281,6:POKE53272,21:REM BORDER,BACKGROUND AND UPPER CASE
40 DIMN(7)
```

```
50 HO$=CHR$(19):CL$=CHR$(147):CD$=CHR$(1
7):BU$=CHR$(31):WH$=CHR$(5)
60 GR$=CHR$(30):RD$=CHR$(28):R1$=CHR$(18
):R0$=CHR$(146):LB$=CHR$(154)
70 S$="                                                        ":S4$=LEFT$(S$,14)
80 S1=54273:S2=54272:VL=54296:WV=54276:A
D=54277:SR=54278:REM SOUND VARIABLES
90 PRINTCL$;WH$;
100 REM
110 REM DRAW SPACE SHIP & GROUND
120 REM
130 HT=1:CO$=WH$
140 GOSUB560
150 PRINTGR$;:FORK=1TO14:PRINTCD$;:NEXT
160 FORK=1TO279:PRINTCHR$(166);:NEXT
170 POKE56295,5:POKE2023,102
180 REM
190 REM GENERATE NOTES
200 REM
210 FORJ=1TO7
220 FORL=1TOJ
230 N(L)=INT(8*RND(1)+1)
240 IFL=1THENGOTO260
250 IFN(L)=N(L-1)THENGOTO230
260 NT=N(L):GOSUB690
270 NEXTL
280 REM
290 REM PLAY NOTES
300 REM
310 EI=0
320 I=140
330 FORK=1TOJ
340 GETI$:IFI$="G"ORI$="S"OR(I$>="1"ANDI
$<="9")THENGOTO360
350 I=I+1:GOSUB650:GOTO340
360 IFI$="G"THENK=J:GOTO400
370 IFI$="S"THENGOSUB860:K=1:GOTO340
380 NT=(VAL(I$)):GOSUB690
390 IFVAL(I$)<>N(K)THENEI=1
400 NEXTK
410 IFI$="G"THENGOTO220
```

```
420 IFEI=0THENCO$=BU$:GOSUB560:HT=HT+2:C
O$=WH$:GOSUB560:GOSUB820:GOTO440
430 GOTO310
440 NEXTJ
450 REM
460 REM EXPLOSION
470 REM
480 POKEVL,15:POKEAD,25:POKESR,246:POKES
2,12:POKEWV,129
490 FORK=10TO60:POKES1,N:NEXT
500 FORI=1TO100:POKE53281,2:FORT=1TO50:N
EXT
510 POKE53281,7:FORT=1TO50:NEXTT
520 NEXTI
530 POKEWV,0:POKEVL,0:POKEAD,0:POKESR,0
540 GOTO890
550 REM
560 REM SPACE-SHIP SUBROUTINE
570 PRINTHO$;:FORI=1TOHT:PRINTCD$;:NEXT
580 IFCO$=WH$THENR$=R1$:G1$=CHR$(169):G2
$=CHR$(127):GOTO600
590 R$=R0$:G1$=" ":G2$=" "
600 PRINTCO$;R0$;
610 PRINTS4$;R$;G1$;"              ";G2$
620 PRINTLEFT$(S$,7);R$;"
             "
630 PRINTS4$;G2$;R$;"              ";R0$;G1$
640 RETURN
650 REM LIGHTS SUBROUTINE
660 IFI>=25THENPOKE782,31:POKE781,HT+1:S
YS65520:PRINTWH$;R1$;" ";:I=1
670 POKE782,6+I:POKE781,HT+1:SYS65520:PR
INTWH$;R1$;" ";RD$;" ";
680 RETURN
690 REM PLAY SUBROUTINE
700 POKEVL,15:POKEAD,190:POKEWV,33
710 IFNT=1THENPOKES1,34:POKES2,75
720 IFNT=2THENPOKES1,38:POKES2,126
730 IFNT=3THENPOKES1,43:POKES2,52
740 IFNT=4THENPOKES1,45:POKES2,198
750 IFNT=5THENPOKES1,51:POKES2,97
```

```
760 IFNT=6THENPOKES1,57:POKES2,172
770 IFNT=7THENPOKES1,64:POKES2,188
780 IFNT=8THENPOKES1,68:POKES2,149
790 FORTT=1TO200:NEXTTT
800 POKEWV,0:POKEVL,0:POKEAD,0
810 RETURN
820 REM ROTATE SUBROUTINE
830 GOSUB860
840 FORD=1TO50:I=I+1:GOSUB650:NEXTD
850 RETURN
860 REM FLUSH SUBROUTINE
870 FORL=S2TOS2+24:POKEL,0:NEXT
880 RETURN
890 END
```

WIRE MAZE

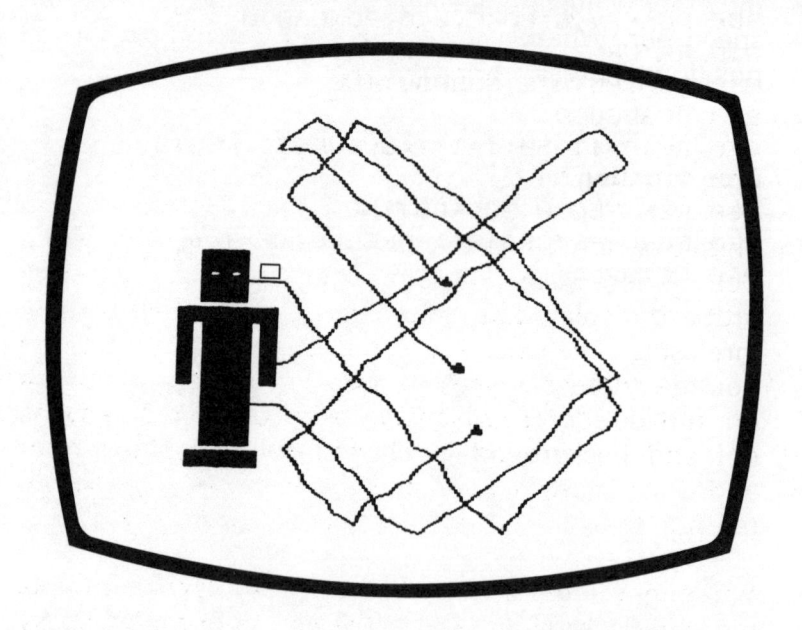

Well at last you have your own robot to cut the grass, clean the car, wash the windows and take the dog for a walk. There is one snag, however.

Your robot has been wired up incorrectly. It must have been Friday afternoon when the other robots put your model together. At the moment, if you press the arm-control button the robot's legs move. You, I'm afraid, are going to have to rewire your new family friend.

How to play

You trace out the wires using the white sticky labels engineers use. When you have positioned white labels at the beginning and end of the same wire press Return. A high note indicates that you are right and a low note tune indicates you are wrong. The program will place a white label on one end of each wire in turn and you can move the other white label between the wires by pressing the space bar. When you are satisfied that it is correctly positioned, press Return.

Programming hints

This program uses the high-resolution facility of the Commodore 64 and includes some useful subroutines. In order to display dots on the screen you need to know three sets of values. That is, the X, Y co-ordinates of the dot, the address which has to be POKEd to turn the dot on, and the address which has to be POKEd to display the dot and background in chosen colours. The former addresses start at 8192 and the latter at 1024 so are referred to by these numbers in the REM statements.

You might find the wire maze too easy. It can be made more difficult by increasing the length of each wire by increasing the larger number in line 410.

Program

```
10 REM WIRE MAZE
20 REM COPYRIGHT (C) G.LUDINSKI 1983
30 DIMXA(3)
40 DIMYA(3)
50 DIMW(3),Z(3),A(3),TB(3)
60 POKE53280,2:POKE53281,12:REM BORDER,B
ACKGROUND
70 HO$=CHR$(19):CL$=CHR$(147):CG$=CHR$(1
51)
80 PRINTCL$;CG$;
90 S1=54273:S2=54272:VL=54296:WV=54276:A
D=54277:SR=54278:REM SOUND VARIABLES
100 FORK=S2TOS2+24:POKEK,0:NEXT
110 REM
```

```
120 REM DRAW ROBOT
130 REM
140 BE$="":FORK=1TO40:BE$=BE$+"E":NEXT
150 B2$=LEFT$(BE$,27)
160 PRINTCL$;:PRINTBE$;BE$;BE$;BE$;
170 PRINT"EEEEE11111EEE";B2$;:PRINT"EEEE
E10101EEE";B2$;
180 FORK=1TO2:PRINT"EEEEE11111EEE";B2$;:
NEXT
190 FORK=1TO2:PRINT"EE77777777777";B2$;:
NEXT
200 FORK=1TO6:PRINT"EE77E77777E77";B2$;:
NEXT
210 FORK=1TO5:PRINT"EEEEE11111EEE";B2$;:
NEXT
220 PRINT"EEE111111111E";B2$;
230 PRINTBE$;BE$;BE$;BE$;LEFT$(BE$,39);:
POKE2023,5
240 GOSUB850:GOSUB900:GOSUB1190:GOTO270
250 GOSUB850
260 FORY=960+8192TO5764+8192STEP320:FORX
=112TO320:POKEX+Y,0:NEXT:NEXT
270 XA(1)=112:YA(1)=30:XA(2)=112:YA(2)=8
5:XA(3)=112:YA(3)=130
280 REM
290 REM DECIDE WHICH LABEL IS DISPLAYED
FIRST
300 REM
310 FORI=1TO3
320 W(I)=INT(RND(1)*3+1)
330 IF(I=2ANDW(I)=W(1))OR(I=3AND(W(I)=W(
2)ORW(I)=W(1)))THENGOTO320
340 NEXTI
350 REM
360 REM DRAW WIRES
370 REM
380 FORI=1TO3
390 IFI<>2THENXS=(-1)↑INT(RND(1)*2):YS=(
-1)↑INT(RND(1)*2):GOTO410
400 YS=-YS
410 FORJ=1TO150
```

```
420 DX=XS
430 RR=INT(RND(1)*100+100)
440 IF((XA(I)+DX)<112OR(XA(I)+DX)>200)OR
XA(I)=RRTHENXS=-XS:GOTO420
450 XA(I)=XA(I)+DX
460 DY=YS
470 RR=INT(RND(1)*100+32)
480 IF((YA(I)+DY)<25OR(YA(I)+DY)>140)ORY
A(I)=RRTHENYS=-YS:GOTO460
490 YA(I)=YA(I)+DY
500 X=XA(I):Y=YA(I):GOSUB1040:Z(I)=Z
510 NEXTJ
520 NEXTI
530 REM
540 REM DRAW LABELS
550 REM
560 FORI=1TO3
570 ZB=Z(I)
580 GOSUB980
590 A(I)=AZ
600 POKEA(I),2
610 NEXT
620 REM
630 REM WRITE QUESTIONS
640 REM
650 FORI=1TO3:GOSUB680:NEXT
660 FORK=1TO3:POKEA(K),5:POKETB(K),5:NEX
T
670 GOTO250
680 REM QUESTION SUBROUTINE
690 IFI=1THENX=90:Y=30:GOSUB930:ZB=Z:GOS
UB980:TB(1)=AZ:POKETB(1),1
700 IFI<>2THENGOTO720
710 X=106:Y=85:GOSUB930:ZB=Z:GOSUB980:TB
(2)=AZ:POKETB(2),1
720 IFI<>3THENGOTO740
730 X=90:Y=130:GOSUB930:ZB=Z:GOSUB980:TB
(3)=AZ:POKETB(3),1
740 T=W(I):POKEA(T),1
750 GETAN$:IFAN$<>" "ANDAN$<>CHR$(13)THE
NGOTO750
```

```
760 IFAN$=CHR$(13)THENGOTO810
770 POKEA(T),2
780 T=T+1:IFT>3THENT=1
790 POKEA(T),1
800 GOTO750
810 IFT=ITHENGOSUB1080:GOTO830
820 GOSUB1130
830 FORK=1TO3:POKEA(K),2:POKETB(K),5:NEXT
840 RETURN
850 REM HI-RES SUBROUTINE
860 POKE53272,(PEEK(53272)OR8)
870 POKE51,255:POKE55,255:POKE52,31:POKE56,31
880 POKE53265,PEEK(53265)OR32
890 RETURN
900 REM BLANK SCREEN SUBROUTINE
910 FORN=8192TO8192+8000:POKEN,0:NEXT
920 RETURN
930 REM X,Y TO 8192 SUBROUTINE
940 Y1=INT(Y/8):Y2=8*((Y/8)-Y1)
950 X1=INT(X/8):PX=7-(8*((X/8)-X1))
960 Z=((Y1*320)+(X1*8)+Y2)+8192
970 RETURN
980 REM 8192 TO 1024 SUBROUTINE
990 ZZ=ZB-8192
1000 YZ=INT(ZZ/320)
1010 XZ=INT((ZZ-(YZ*320))/8)
1020 AZ=1024+(YZ*40)+XZ
1030 RETURN
1040 REM DRAW DOT AT X,Y SUBROUTINE
1050 GOSUB930
1060 POKEZ,PEEK(Z)OR2↑PX
1070 RETURN
1080 REM RIGHT SOUND SUBROUTINE
1090 POKEWV,33:POKEVL,15:POKEAD,190:POKESR,248
1100 POKES1,68:POKES2,149:FORTT=1TO400:NEXTTT
1110 POKEWV,0:POKEVL,0:POKEAD,0:POKESR,0
1120 RETURN
```

```
1130 REM WRONG SOUND SUBROUTINE
1140 POKEWV,33:POKEVL,15:POKEAD,190:POKE
SR,248
1150 POKES1,45:POKES2,198:FORTT=1TO300:N
EXTTT
1160 POKES1,43:POKES2,52:FORTT=1TO300:NE
XTTT
1170 POKEWV,0:POKEVL,0:POKEAD,0:POKESR,0
1180 RETURN
1190 REM DRAW WIRE TOPS SUBROUTINE
1200 Y=30:FORX=80TO112:GOSUB1040:NEXT
1210 Y=85:FORX=100TO112:GOSUB1040:NEXT
1220 Y=130:FORX=80TO112:GOSUB1040:NEXT
1230 RETURN
```

ALSO AVAILABLE FROM
PHOENIX

THE
COMMODORE 64
PROGRAM BOOK

Here is a blockbusting collection
of adventures, games and utilities
to exploit the colour and graphics at your command.

The adventures
will test your powers of logic and deduction
as you seek treasure in "Forbidden City" and "Pharaoh's Curse".

There is a wide selection of
arcade-style games
plus a Flight Simulation game which will test
your reactions to the full.

The utilities
include, for budding programmers,
a highly versatile assembler/disassembler
and a line renumber program.

This is
"the" Commodore 64 Program Book
with something for everyone.

AVAILABLE
from all
good book shops

£5.95

PHOENIX
Publishing Associates
14 Vernon Road Bushey
Hertfordshire WD2 2JL
or direct
£5.95 plus 50p p/p